Environmental Foundations
of
European History

Environmental Foundations
of European History

by

DERWENT WHITTLESEY

Professor of Geography
Harvard University

NEW YORK

APPLETON-CENTURY-CROFTS, INC.

Preface

This book began with a request I received in 1939. It came from the group teaching Medieval and Modern European history at Harvard University. One of the renowned courses in the college, "History One," was headed by the late Professor Roger B. Merriman with the collaboration of Messrs. John M. Potter, subsequently President of Hobart College, and Paul Cram, assisted by a staff of about a dozen young scholars aflame with zeal for the tutorial conference method as a touchstone of college education. These men wanted material for outside reading, to give the class some understanding of the geography of Europe, and to serve as a springboard for conferences with the sections into which the five hundred members of the course were divided, and incidentally, in tutorial sessions with individuals.

They turned to me not only as a geographic colleague, but also because I had originally planned to follow history as a profession, and had taught it for a year, besides completing a historical dissertation. Geography had come to my attention and stirred my interest while I was in the graduate school, because it built a solid foundation beneath my historical studies. Thereafter the separation between the two subjects in the American college curriculum seemed to me unnatural and wasteful in contrast to the logical practice of French universities, where the serious student of either subject is required to study both. When the American custom of separating my two fields of study compelled me to make the hard choice between them, the center of my interest remained in the

[v]

border field where they overlap. I therefore welcomed the opportunity, after twenty years as a practicing geographer, to prepare, for supplementary reading in the study of European history, a survey of the relevant geography.

During several months I worked on a manuscript which every member of the History One staff studied and then criticized in conferences that included the whole group. After each discussion I revised the manuscript to embody the suggestions made by the men who would be using the material. Meanwhile, maps I devised to illustrate the text were designed and drawn by Mr. Rowland Illick. Then the text was mimeographed, with citations to William R. Shepherd's *Historical Atlas* as partial substitutes for my maps, not reproduced at that time because of the cost. That coverless typescript in three parts I copyrighted in 1940. It comprised the bulk of Chapters 2, 3, and 4, and the Prolog of the present volume, and continued to be used for several years by the Harvard classes. A plan to publish it, with some additions, under the Crofts imprint had to be shelved because for nearly a decade war work and its aftermath absorbed all the time I could spare from the allotted teaching of geography.

A year or so ago the question of publication was again raised. Since 1940, the script had received the benefit of testing in successive classes, and now could also be scrutinized in the perspective of eight years of crucial history. On rereading, the core of the study appeared to be as relevant as when it was written for use in history classes, and to be equally applicable in courses dealing more broadly with Western Civilization. It stands unchanged apart from numerous but minor revisions and a few amplifying paragraphs. The maps I originally designed were on hand, ready to replace the makeshift references to Shepherd's *Atlas*. It seemed desirable to add two sections, both of which had been proposed during the original discussions: a new Chapter 1, to lay environmental foundations for courses that survey Ancient History as well as the later eras; and a final chapter, here numbered 5, to take stock of the geography of contemporary Europe, in an era of change that appears to be as sweeping and fundamental as those critical periods for which the three original chapters present the settings. These supplements, together with accompanying maps (also drawn by Mr. Illick), round out a picture of sequent European geography in which each

[vi]

stage is conceived as the set for one of the grand epochs of European history.

In courses that begin with Medieval History, Chapter 1 may be omitted, although it has pertinence, especially for Modern History, since the Mediterranean World it delineates has come once again entirely within the theater of European history. Surveys of Western Civilization appropriately begin with the area discussed in Chapter 1.

Chapter 5 is a view of Europe as the contemporary product of events and environment. It undertakes to lay a reliable foundation for individual pursuit of history-in-the-making—the items usually called current events.

As is true of any geographic study, the maps in the book are as important as the text. Each map is inserted at the point of first use, and for easy reference, subsequent citations give the page as well as the figure number. It is assumed that a historical atlas is available to the student. The data of the historical maps in the atlas will often be given fresh meaning if compared with geographic maps in this volume.

Suggestions for further use of geographic materials and tools in the study of European history, both individually and in the classroom, will be found in the Appendix.

Some readers may object to the emphasis on material technology, and the omission of reference to the inner life of mankind implied in the word "spiritual." The cause of this imbalance is the occasion for the book: as a rule European histories, and particularly textbooks, deal at length with the intellectual and spiritual aspects of human societies, but neglect or omit the earth basis of human existence and progression. This book is intended to fill the gap, so far as can be done by describing briefly successive stages on which the drama of European life has been played, and indicating the significance of the natural conditions at each stage in the sequence. The actors and their acts are properly left to the texts which I hope this book will serve as a useful supplement.

D. W.

Harvard University

Contents

CONTENTS

CONTENTS

List of Maps

[xiii]

Environmental Foundations
of
European History

"Europe," a Historical Designation

Just what and where is Europe? Maps usually show it as the huge peninsula that projects westward from the main land mass of the Eurasian continent (Fig. 2, p. 6). They are likely to draw its eastern limit along the Ural Mountains, the Ural River, and the Caspian Sea, but the exact borderline is often shown as running eastward of the southern Ural Mountains, and well to the west of the Ural River. Since the 17th century, every such boundary has cut squarely through Russian territory. Since the Russian Revolution of 1917, and increasingly since World War II, this traditional line has lost any reality it may once have had. Perhaps it is too early to determine the merits of other possible eastern boundaries for Europe in the unsettled contemporary world. This very difficulty highlights the significant fact—that the area and boundaries of "Europe" have always been in flux and are not now fixed.

EUROPE IN THE EARTH'S LARGEST LAND MASS

As a continental mass, the whole of Eurasia is a single unit, and Africa is a further extension of it. In most aspects of its physical geography, the western parts of Asia and the north coast of Africa more closely resemble Europe than the vast remainders of the continents to which they belong. The archeological and historical record of human life shows repeated intermingling and migration

[1]

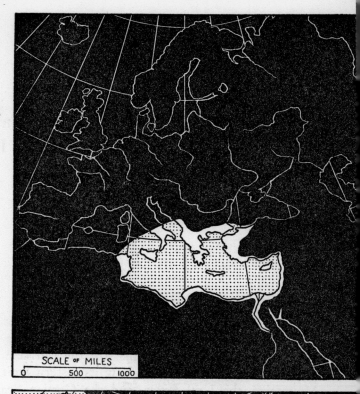

EUROPE
ABOUT 1000 B.C.

EUROPE
ABOUT 1000 A.D.

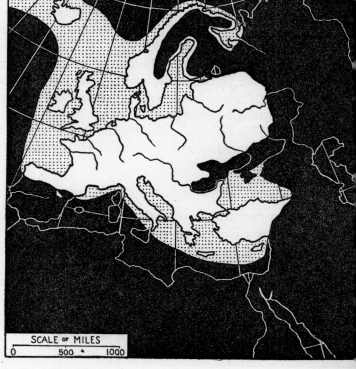

1 C

FIG. 1. EUROPE AT

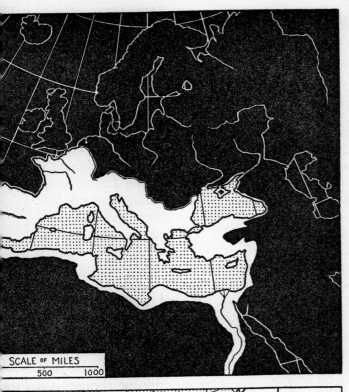

Europe at About
the Beginning of
the Christian Era

SCALE of MILES
500   1000

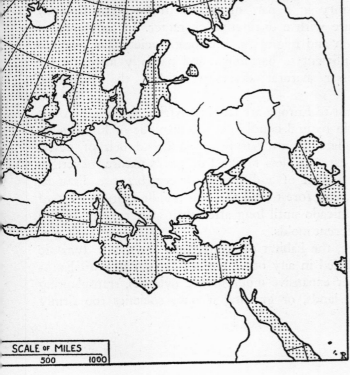

Europe Today

SCALE of MILES
500   1000

1 D

INTERVALS OF 1000 YEARS.

between Europe, Asia, and Africa. Unimpeachable written records trace the course of Western civilization in unbroken lineage from societies settled at the eastern end of the Mediterranean Sea—an area comprising parts of all three continents.

The sweep of western society from small beginnings is suggested by the maps (Fig. 1, p. 2) of arbitrary points in history a thousand years apart (dating back from our own time). They show that only a tiny corner of the physical continent of Europe figured in the civilized world three thousand years ago—the Greek fringe of broken peninsulas and off-shore islands reaching toward Asia. A thousand years later the entire Mediterranean Basin, but very little of the European land north of it, had been brought into the orbit of civilization. Expansion northward and eastward was slow throughout the next millennium and a half. During this long period the eastern boundary of "Europe" fluctuated with expanding European society. In recent centuries, the Ural mountain range has been taken as the demarcation, perhaps chiefly because it is the only break in the uniform interior of northern Eurasia that shows on an ordinary map.

In reality the boundary is unimportant, compared to the fact that Europe has achieved the status of a continent through the operation of history in a part of the earth (western Eurasia) stamped by nature with a distinctive character. In thousands of years of expansion and migration, European society has acquired distinctiveness sufficient to harmonize and partially integrate the marked but lesser natural diversity within the European "continent."

In sharp contrast to Europe are tropical Africa and South Asia—totally different in natural conditions and in mode of life, besides being sharply isolated from Europe by a broad belt of desert (Fig. 2, p. 6). East Asia, less unlike Europe in nature, nevertheless became the habitat of a different society, because distance, desert, mountain, and forest held the two middle-latitude ends of Eurasia incommunicado until long after their patterns of life had become set in different molds.

Europe is, then, the habitat of western civilization, a dynamic society not paralleled in any other part of the earth, until Europeans carried their expansive mode of life overseas, transplanting it to unoccupied lands, or grafting it onto societies too firmly

[4]

rooted to be dislodged. The interaction of place and people that brought about the unique society known as "western," is a principal concern of European history. This book undertakes to sketch the successive settings of natural conditions upon which society has traced the pattern of human life, in the principal seats of European history.

EUROPE IN THE STREAM OF HUMAN SETTLEMENT

Each historical epoch traces its own distinctive pattern upon the earth surface. The most visible evidences are items of material culture. In the process the original natural environment is modified while the conditions of nature are helping to shape the cultural landscape. Put differently, each habitat poses problems for its denizens, problems they undertake to solve with the means at their command. These means include tools and weapons—items that vary with the stage of material technology. Equally important devices are modes of organization: economic practices, social attitudes, and the political order. The character of the imprint traced upon the earth, and the depth of its etching, vary with the effectiveness of all these implements, and with the plasticity of the conditioning natural environment.

With every marked change in material and social technology, and with every expansion into a fresh environment, the imprint upon the landscape changes its pattern and character. The fresh impress may deepen the old lines or it may efface them, but usually it leaves part of the older pattern while superimposing a new design. The resulting tracery may be understandingly read only if the succession of impressions is recognized.

The major epochs of European history, viewed as successive patterns of natural-cultural landscape, are the subjects of the chapters that follow. As time has advanced from the remote past toward the present day, the periods have become shorter and the patterns more complex. This is so partly because more is known about recent times than about eras long past. But in addition, the tempo of human life is increasing with every basic change in technology and society, and the earth's resources are being used in ever greater variety.

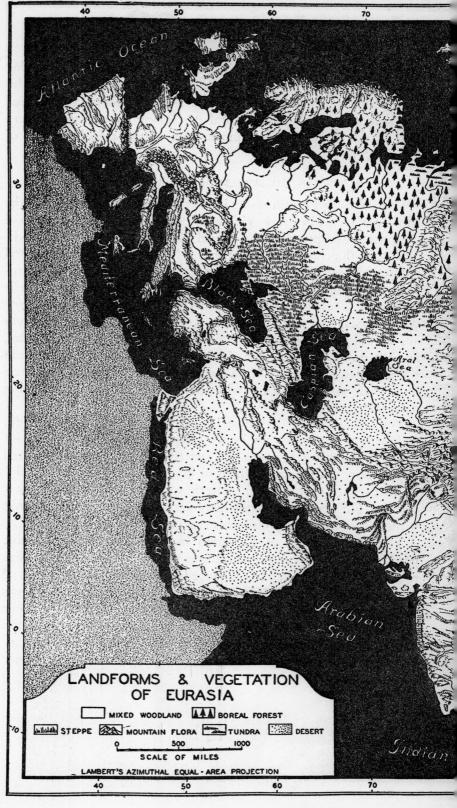

LANDFORMS & VEGETATION
OF EURASIA

MIXED WOODLAND   BOREAL FOREST

STEPPE   MOUNTAIN FLORA   TUNDRA   DESERT

0   500   1000
SCALE OF MILES

LAMBERT'S AZIMUTHAL EQUAL-AREA PROJECTION

FIG. 2. LANDFORMS AND

VEGETATION OF EURASIA.

CHAPTER I

The Anterooms of European History

Until after 1000 B.C., European history was confined to the lands at and near the eastern end of the Mediterranean Sea (Fig. 1a, p. 2). The earliest of the societies to have left written records did not face that Sea, nor did they live in the continent that has come to be known as Europe. They belong none the less to the history of Europe, because they made initial and fundamental contributions to the successive expanding peoples and modes of life that moved westward and northward to create the Europe of today.

CONTRASTING HABITATS OF THE EASTERN MEDITERRANEAN REGION

All the southerly margin of the European world is marked by dry climates. Indeed, the farthest limit of the European habitat is a broad belt of desert, where rain is both scanty and unreliable (Fig. 2, p. 6). Again and again peoples of the desert have participated in or interfered with European affairs. A few favored spots within the desert have figured as anterooms to the theater of European history.

Between undeniable desert and the always humid lands of northern Europe lies a belt of transition, where the summer is almost or quite rainless, and the year's modest total precipitation falls as rain during the cooler season. This peculiar climate borders

[8]

the Mediterranean Sea, and is often called the Mediterranean climate.

European, or Western, society germinated in the deserts and the coastlands at and near the eastern end of the Mediterranean. As seedbeds for European flowering, their contrasting characters deserve brief consideration.

The Deserts

In the desert and its semi-arid margins the undependable rainfall confines fixed settlements to the cramped spots where surface or underground water accumulates. There the population is dense because of the reliable and intensive agricultural output made possible by fertile soil, everyday sunshine, and judicious use of water to irrigate the crops. Small groups of herdsfolk rove over the remaining vast spaces in pursuit of ephemeral vegetation and temporary water supplies.

Conditions therefore favor two opposite modes of living, sedentary and nomadic, reciprocal in products and often organized as commensal or complementary social groups. Life is concentrated upon the rare pools or waterholes and the still rarer streams, and turns away from the sea.

Egypt. In the part of the Eastern Mediterranean region that has come to be known as the continent of Africa, the irrigable valley of the Lower Nile made the base for the earliest compact and powerful social group in the entire western world. This "cradle of civilization" was the "gift of the Nile" because the lower valley of that stream was uniquely favorable to an early sedentary society.

A narrow valley threaded by a navigable waterway was protected from human enemies by waterless desert, except at the ends (Fig. 3, p. 10). In the north, a marshy delta was passable only by way of shifting channels of the river and across bars at their mouths; in the south, rapids and gorges in barren desert halted movement by water and discouraged overland travel. The valley's flat floor was built up of fertile soil washed from the volcanic uplands of distant Ethiopia. For a few months, once a year, torrential rains on this highland gathered in a flood mighty enough to cross the Sahara and irrigate the river floodplain by natural overflow. Lakes and marshes still farther upstream than the source of the floods, kept full by all-year rains, maintained the Lower

[9]

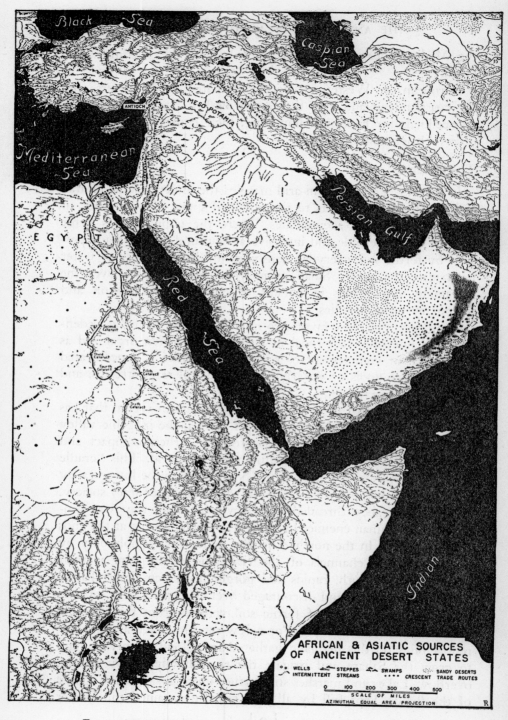

FIG. 3. AFRICAN AND ASIATIC SOURCES OF ANCIENT
DESERT STATES.

[10]

Nile at a moderate level between floods. When trade brought Egypt into contact with the outside world, the country profited as middleman by using the gently-flowing Nile as a water link between the Mediterranean and Red seas. Itself a product of natural conditions found in Africa and not in Europe, Ancient Egypt nevertheless came to have close connections with Europe and contributed much to the society that is called "western" or "occidental."

Mesopotamia. On the desert margin of Western Asia lies Mesopotamia, a "land between rivers" that afforded an oasis base for a succession of states roughly contemporary with the Egyptian empires (Fig. 3, p. 10). Its irrigable land, like Egypt's, was set apart by desert and delta, but less sharply. The rivers, fed by mountain torrents, could carry shipping only at high water and downstream. Nevertheless, Mesopotamia has always been a link in the overland connection between Europe and the Near and Middle East, one of the earliest and most persistent trade routes on earth. Traffic paralleled the rivers on the plain itself; farther upstream, where the rivers descend from their mountain sources, the trade route followed the oasis-dotted piedmont that sweeps in a crescent to the Mediterranean shore, bounded by rugged Asia Minor on the north and waterless desert on the south.

The irrepressible commerce of this route enriched the Mesopotamian peoples, and also embroiled them in recurrent warfare. In both peace and war they bombarded the adjacent Mediterranean coastlands with their ways and views of life, thereby making important contributions to European society of contemporary and later epochs.

The Seacoasts

The Mediterranean coast has been conspicuously associated with maritime peoples, but not all parts of it have been inhabited by seafarers. Both east and west of Egypt nomadic bands followed their flocks to the water's edge, but made no use of the water. This paradox of physical nearness and functional remoteness rested on a combination of natural conditions—unirrigable coastal desert and lack of harbors (Fig. 4, p. 12). Rainier and more indented coastlines were the early sites of maritime settlements. They became centers for a sedentary society of farmer-fisher-trader folk that

[11]

FIG. 4. RELIEF AND CLIMATE

The map itself contains the following labels:

North Atlantic Ocean

North Sea

Bay Of Biscay

ROME

RELIEF AND CLIMATE
OF THE ROMAN EMPIRE

Mediterranean   Highland   Continental Long Summer
Marine West Coast   Desert   Continental Short Summer
Semi-Arid   Subpolar   Lower High Latitude
- - - - - Greatest Extent of Roman Empire

0   100   200   400   600
SCALE OF MILES
CONIC PROJECTION

OF THE ROMAN EMPIRE.

spread into festoons of settlements on all the more favored coast-lands of the inland seas.

The mild Mediterranean winters were rainy enough to permit crop-growing except in the southeast and to provide pasturage on lands too hilly for tillage. Marshlands (mainly on coastal plains) furnished summer forage. The dry summers were mitigated by supplemental irrigation where streams or seepage made water available. Flocks and irrigated lands gave the coastal folk something in common with the desert dwellers, although the farming systems were basically different, thanks to the occurrence of winter rains in the one habitat, and the absence of a rainy season in the other.

Timber was scarce, except on the highest mountains, and was reserved for shipbuilding, furniture, and roof timbers. Good building stone was readily available everywhere except in a few large alluvial lowlands, chiefly Egypt, Mesopotamia, and the Po Plain. There clay for brickmaking was easily obtained.

Copper, lead, iron, and silver were found in small but adequate amounts. Tin, gold, and amber dribbled in from places outside the Mediterranean Basin.

Variety of produce from place to place, due to diversity of land-forms and consequent variation in local climate and in soil, encouraged exchange. Early saturation on the restricted resources of any one small territorial base spurred people to look abroad for supplements. Trade was facilitated by the nearby sea—calm in summer and not tempestuous for long even in winter. The coastal settlements differed radically from those of the interior in that they could live in part by seaborne trade. As a consequence commercial cities became dominant and stamped Mediterranean society with a truly maritime character.

The Mediterranean seacoasts vary greatly in detail, but most sections are notably indented, and islands large and small are numerous. Hills or mountains rise abruptly from the sea. Where ranges parallel the coast they may leave little or no lowland; where they end in promontories, intermontane valleys provide farmland and harbors. The two maritime peoples who took the lead in early Mediterranean trade faced different opportunities and problems through contrasting conditions of their habitats.

Phoenicia. Where the crescent trade route from Mesopotamia and the Orient debouched upon the eastern end of the Mediterranean, the Phoenicians set up as middlemen between Asia and Europe (Figs. 3, p. 10, and 4, p. 12). Their habitable land was the narrow foot of a mountain-range that plunged into the sea. They located their trading towns where islands or reefs could serve as partial protection for their fleets. With their ships they followed the African coast to Gibraltar, and thence along both shores of the Iberian Peninsula. They set up trading stations that stood as islands of settlement between the sea itself and the barren wilderness of the desert interior. Their lives were spent on the sea or very close to it, supported by the trade in wares of the East and frontier goods of the western Mediterranean region.

Greece. Farther north, the coastlands of Asia Minor and of peninsular Greece on the opposite shore of the island-studded Aegean Sea, were settled by seafaring Hellenes. Their early home-lands were small lowlands facing sheltered bays between the cliffed ends of mountain-ranges that cross the region, mainly in an east-west direction. These valleys were moister than the Phoenician coast, and therefore more productive, but they had no direct contact with the crescent trade route to Mesopotamia. From the Aegean, centrally located in the eastern Mediterranean area, Hellenic trade and settlement pushed outward in several directions—to the Black Sea, lower Italy and the nearby large islands, and Gaul. Traders and colonists pioneered not only the northern shore of the great inland sea, but also made close contacts with Egypt.

The Phoenician and Hellenic settlements between them came to monopolize all the reaches of the Mediterranean coast that provided harbors as a basis for commerce. Their active trade and the small size of the farmlands surrounding the trading towns emphasized the urban character of each of the many independent "city states" and of Mediterranean society as a whole.

MEDITERRANEAN UNIFICATION

Competition for the seaborne trade was one root of constant quarrels between the numerous small sovereign states that dotted the coasts. The celebrated ten-year conflict between Troy in Asia Minor and city-states of the Greek Peninsula was typical. Its object was control of the entrance to the Hellespont (Dardanelles), and consequent dominance of the lucrative frontier trade of the Black Sea (Fig. 4, p. 12). Several trading cities of peninsular Greece

[15]

joined forces to win this rich prize, but characteristically they broke up their alliance as soon as they obtained it.

Less frequent were epic struggles that occurred when strongly based inland states overran their maritime neighbors in the course of seaward expansion. In one such encounter, the Persian army had to retreat in the face of superior naval force marshalled by an alliance of Greek city states. In contrast, Rome, originally a land-minded state of central Italy, dominated the Hellenic coastal settlements of that peninsula, and then wrested control of the western basin of the Mediterranean from Phoenician Carthage in a bitter conflict that took for its war-cry: "Cartago delenda est." It is significant that Rome remained paramount as a landpower while gaining mastery of the sea.

The geographic evolution of the Ancient Mediterranean world consisted of uniting the seafaring coastal units with the inland centers. A degree of unity was finally imposed upon the whole area by Rome, operating from a position in the middle of the Mediterranean world. Roman dominance created political unity in an area of moderate natural and cultural diversity, and varying degrees of economic and social integration followed.

Ultimately, Roman territory reached beyond the dry coastlands and the desert oases, to climates both cool and humid (Fig. 4, p. 12). This was an expansion into the continent of Europe, and had lasting effects on subsequent European history. Throughout Roman times, however, the conquered humid lands remained marginal to the Mediterranean coreland of Classical Antiquity.[1]

[1] Further details of the Mediterranean landscape pattern are presented on pp. 21-22 and 26-28.

CHAPTER II

Europe on the Threshold
of the Middle Ages

A TRIPARTITE ENTITY

The Europe of the Middle Ages over-
lapped the Europe of Classical Antiquity,
but also it spread over new territory and
lost area that had traditionally belonged to western society (Figs.
1b, p. 3, and 1c, p. 2). The unified state created by ancient Rome
had for its nucleus the Mediterranean Basin (Fig. 4, p. 12). At its
greatest extent (117 A.D.) it had incorporated the irrigated deserts
of African Egypt and Asian Mesopotamia to the south and east
(Fig. 3, p. 10). Northwestward it had spread along the Atlantic
face of Europe to the Scottish Lowland, and it had reached northeast beyond the mountains of central Europe into the Danube
Basin. The Danube and Rhine rivers may be taken as approximate
limits of the Roman state in continental Europe.

The way of life characteristic of the Roman Empire was evolved
mainly in the small valleys and plains of rugged Mediterranean
coastlands. There the impress was sharp and deep, and has never
disappeared. The area of North Europe later annexed presented
different conditions of nature, and strictly Mediterranean life introduced by the Romans was correspondingly modified. The Roman
impress diminished as inaccessibility from the Mediterranean increased, *i. e.*, with distance and rough terrain. Beyond the Roman
political boundaries the land was subjected to Romanization only
at second hand, through trade during Roman times and by penetra-

[17]

TRIPARTITE
MEDIEVAL WORLD

SCALE OF MILES

0   100   200   400   600

CONIC PROJECTION

Fig. 5. THE TRIPARTITE

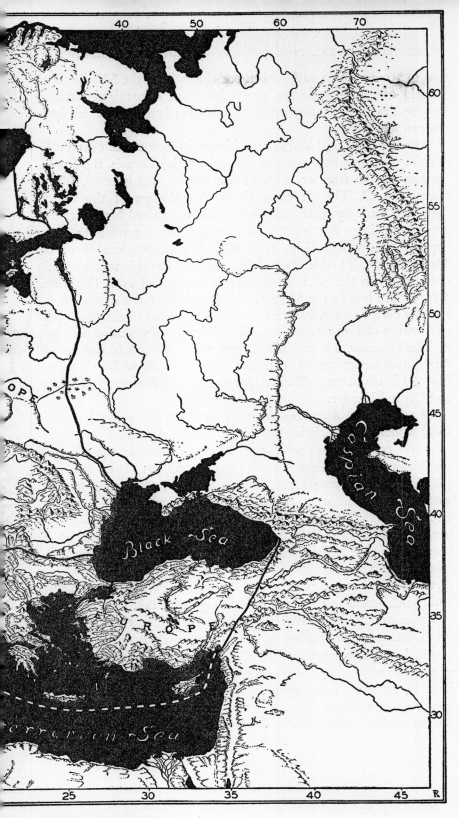

MEDIEVAL WORLD.

tion of Roman ideas and institutions throughout the Middle Ages. Within central Europe the parts closest to Romanized territory absorbed more of Romanesque culture than lands farther away to the east and north.

When the political boundary of imperial Rome was overrun by peoples from northeastern Europe and interior Eurasia, the Roman impress on the frontier lands of the empire was blurred, and in places effaced. Thus it came about that Europe of the Middle Ages was made up of an indigenous and Romanized Mediterranean area, a partially Romanized Northwest, and a remainder never directly Romanized (Fig. 5, p. 18). The preponderance of the Mediterranean in this three-fold medieval world was abruptly reduced when the African and Asian lands, and even Iberia and Sicily, were lost to the Mohammedan culture of the desert nomad and the oasis dweller. Natural conditions pointed to this three-fold subdivision of Europe, and societies of the Ancient period accented it. The boundaries have shifted from epoch to epoch, but critical differences never ceased to trisect the area with which Medieval History is concerned—Mediterranean Europe, Northwest Europe, and Central Europe.

The European Mountain Barrier. At about the millennial mark from which the Christian world dates its calendar, Europe was roughly coterminous with the Mediterranean coastlands and closely associated hinterlands (Fig. 1b, p. 3). This world of Classical Antiquity was the Roman Empire. On the south and east, Roman authority rested against and was limited by an effective barrier—the wide belt of deserts that runs like a heraldic bend sinister across the map of Asia and Africa. On the north its bounds included and in places crossed the barrier zone of mountains that stands disjointedly along the northern margins of the three Mediterranean peninsulas and continues through Anatolia and the Caucasus to the Caspian Sea (Fig. 4, p. 12).

These mountains, unlike the deserts that limit Europe on the south, interpose no continuous bar to the movement of people and goods, but rather constitute hurdles of varying difficulty, a series of ranges and masses—Pyrenees, Massif Central, Alps, Carpathians, Balkans, Anatolia, and Caucasus. Passes are deeply notched in the crest lines of all these ranges. Of the many famous in history, a few are especially celebrated. In the eastern Pyrenees is the Perthus, through which Hannibal led his troops on the way to Rome. In the Alps are the lofty St. Bernard, known for its deep snows and its ministering dogs; the St. Gotthard, a foundation stone of the Swiss nation; the low Brenner, bone of contention between Germanic and Italian peoples from time immemorial to the present. In a few places there are narrow lowland breaches between adjacent mountain groups. Two are especially notable. The Rhône Valley and its connections provide a through route of navigable streams and low divides. The straits connecting the Mediterranean and Black seas constitute a seaway.

Despite these numerous cross routes, the ranges that mark the northern confines of the Mediterranean World do hinder the peacetime movement of people and goods, and figure decisively in military movements. Critical as they have always been in these respects, they have served even more significantly to mark and accentuate a climatic boundary of the first order of magnitude between the Mediterranean coastlands and North Europe.

The Mediterranean Environment

Mediterranean Europe comprises the northern shores of the sea from which it takes its name. A backstop of hills and mountains marks the limit of the region and embraces the many small lowland plains and upland valleys where most of the people live (Figs. 4, p. 12, and 5, p. 18). Ranges and massifs project into the sea to form large peninsulas, and from them jut innumerable headlands and spurs. Numerous islands lie offshore, fragmental crests of mountains half drowned by the sea. Bays and channels indent the mainland coast. In few parts of the world are land and sea so intimately associated. Because the highlands lie nowhere more than a few score miles back from the seashore, small supplies of water from mountain rain and snow are widely available for irrigating coastal lowlands.

Throughout the truly Mediterranean region the summers are rainless, and during the winters the land receives only moderate precipitation. Fortunately this moist season, although cool, is warm enough to permit the growth of crops. The summers are hot; hence crops thrive then too, wherever water to irrigate them is available from stores in the hills and mountains.

Under such conditions of landforms and climate, the arable land, originally lightly wooded or covered with grass, could be turned into farms without preparation beyond the powers of primitive people. The soils, too, have played a helpful part. Thanks to a high lime content, nearly all were fertile to begin with and responded well to careful management. Every winter rivulets from the wooded mountains spread a thin coating of silt on the valley floors and on the gentle alluvial slopes built fanwise along the base of the ranges. This material, originating nearly everywhere in limestones, weathered into fresh, productive soil, retentive of moisture. In consequence, a small acreage of arable land could provide a living for a family in a climate in which plant growth was never halted by prolonged low temperatures. High yields have always permitted the farmer to concentrate on a small holding, and by careful, intensive tillage (deep plowing, frequent weeding, and rotation of crops), to maintain soil fertility.

Natural vegetation typical of the Mediterranean coastlands was a brushy stand of shrubs and low trees, many of which retained leaves throughout the year, but made slow growth. Rainy slopes, particularly those high in the mountains, were originally covered with trees. Flat lands, especially marshes, appear to have been grass covered.

As time passed and population grew, each generation felled a little more of the mountain forests for timber and denuded the lower slopes of brush to burn charcoal or to provide cropland. Then the rains of winter could sweep exposed soil and subsoil off the steep slopes, and swollen torrents, sorting it, carried the finer material out to sea and dumped the coarser part on the alluvial lowlands in the form of gravelly sand. Thus in a single operation of outraged nature, the uplands lost their earth-mantle by erosion and the lowlands lost their fertile soil by burial. With vegetation and soil removed or diminished, the water-storage capacity of the mountains was greatly reduced, to the detriment of irrigation.

Almost everywhere the resulting curtailment of the amount of arable land and the diminished productivity of that which remained were twin evils that increased as the period of Classical Antiquity gave place to the Middle Ages. The deterioration did not fundamentally alter the mode of life in the Mediterranean World, but it made a poorer habitat for its inhabitants.

The Environment of Northwest Europe

In the part of the Roman Empire to the north of the mountains, natural conditions differed from those in the Mediterranean core of the Roman world (Figs. 2, p. 6; 4, p. 12, and 5, p. 18). The Romans, accustomed to a habitat in which water is critical, and therefore the dominant natural element, found Northwest Europe a strange world, to which they were irresistibly drawn by the opportunities for trade along the expanding frontier—an exchange enhanced by contrast between the Northwest and Mediterranean environments.

To begin with, the scale of the landscape is larger. The plains, instead of being habitable patches of lowland facing the sea, are broad. Many of them lie well inland and are surrounded by belts of hill-land. Most parts of the lowland plains could make contact with the sea only via long, winding riverways. Like the Mediterranean lowlands, the plains of Northwest Europe were widely favored with soils derived from limestone. Such of these soils as were naturally well-drained, had been used for crops since Neolithic times. The Romans found them well adapted to wheat, the staple food crop of Mediterranean peoples. Lowlands with heavier soils could be converted into farmland when the preferred light soils had been preempted, but only at the cost of more labor. Because the heavy soils were unsuitable for wheat, they had to be planted to oats, buckwheat, or forage—crops strange to the newcomers from the Mediterranean climate.

To the difference of landforms and soil were added unfamiliar climate and resultant natural vegetation. Trees originally predominated throughout, most of them being deciduous in winter. Where the stand was light, the woodland had generally been burnt off by prehistoric inhabitants. Dense stands of forest covered much ground when the Romans came in and remained throughout the Middle Ages. Sandlands bearing pines, and reedy marshes occurred here and there. Instead of a rainless and brown summer landscape, the countryside was green and lush at that season. The summer there was not a great deal warmer on the average than winter in the Mediterranean, and was the only season when crops throve. Roman immigrants found the winter uncomfortably chilly and unpleasantly rainy, but not unbearable. On the farms this was the dull season, but it was not cold enough to kill fall-sown wheat, or to deaden the grass, upon which farm animals could browse throughout the year.

The contrast in natural environment between Mediterranean and Northwest Europe was conducive to trade. For Mediterranean wine, olive oil, woolen cloths, parchment, and other luxury goods, the Northwest could exchange forest products—timber, pelts, hair, and beeswax—besides hides, flax, and wheat from the farms. In the cool, moist climate, iron ore was found in scattered bogs, set amid forests which yielded charcoal to smelt it. Far away in the northwest, Cornwall was the only important European source of tin—a necessity in making bronze, upon which the civilized Ancient world still relied for many metallic implements and utensils.

The progress of the Romans into the northwest was smoothed by the broad gap in the mountain barrier between the Pyrenees and the Alps (Fig. 4, p. 12). The *Massif Central* of France stands in this breach, but it leaves open a lowland pathway on either side. The Mediterranean shore of this double opening is almost identical in climate with other Mediterranean coasts of Europe, although it is slightly more subject to storms from the north.

These two lowlands, deeply penetrating the continent, are transitional in climate between southern and northern European types. In keeping with the transition in temperature and rainfall, the soils and the natural vegetation alter by degrees. The south of France provided the Romans with a natural laboratory in which they could learn the lessons necessary for successful settlement of lands still farther to the north and west.

The northernmost boundary the Roman Empire ever reached was drawn near the margin of the crystalline uplands of Britain, known today as the Scottish and Welsh Highlands. There rugged terrain, infertile soils derived from granite and other crystalline rocks, and an eternally cloudy and rainy climate combined to make an environment inhospitable to Mediterranean folk, even after a century of successful domicile in north France and in England.

The Environment of Central Europe

Between the Mediterranean region and Central Europe the mountain barrier is higher, wider, and less completely breached than in the west (Figs. 4, p. 12, and 5, p. 18). Even more important, the Central European habitat is a world apart from that of the Mediterranean coastlands. This the Romans recognized, as is evident from their failure to colonize it effectively.

Eastward of the ranges of low mountains that run from the westernmost Alps almost to the North Sea, continental Europe begins. The change is not abrupt, but it is observable in every aspect of the natural environment. The even-tempered climate of Northwest Europe gives way to the prolonged cold and snow of continental winters, and the briefer, although often intense, warmth of continental summers—in other words, the characteristic climate of inland areas in these rather high latitudes. Likewise the plains increase in size and the hills diminish in elevation and in continuity. Fertile soils on limestones become rare. Nearly everywhere north of the Alps and the Carpathians sandy dumps from the last continental ice-sheet cover wide expanses of the lowlands with either a disordered array of hills and hollows left by the retreating ice itself, or with broad sandflats spread out by water from the melting ice-front.

In this colder climate and on this sandier soil, natural vegetation of deciduous woodland gave way progressively to dense and somber forests of spruce, pine, and other coniferous trees (*cf*. Fig. 2, p. 6). Natural openings in the forest occurred mainly in the marshy, impassible valleys of streams and on sandy heaths exposed to bitter winter winds. Only in the southeast—in the Middle and Lower Danube basins of Hungary and Rumania—did forest give way to natural grassland, and copious rains at every season to drier weather reminiscent of the Mediterranean climate. Yet even there the contrasts were considerable. These plains are far larger than typical lowland basins south of the Alps and Balkans. Sandland and marsh cover wide tracts. The temperature is more extreme and uncertain, the cold winters are drier than the long, hot summers. There is no dependably recurrent season of drouth.

Although Northwest Europe was for the Romans a novel world, they did succeed in establishing themselves over most of it. Central Europe posed problems they never solved, except partially and for a short period, along the Rhine and in the Danubian lowlands.

Their failure to conquer and occupy the lands beyond the Rhine and the Danube (except for its lower basin) accentuated and reinforced the natural differentiation between Northwest and North

Central Europe by overlaying it with a pronounced cultural contrast of the first magnitude and of decisive historical importance. The cultural distinction was sharply drawn along the political frontier of the Empire. To be sure, this frontier was a fluctuating line, but for a long time it corresponded roughly to the Rhine and Danube rivers.

After "barbarians" from beyond the frontier succeeded in breaking through the Rhine-Danube boundary, Roman culture lost ground. It was nearly effaced in the exposed border zone north and east of the protective barriers of mountain which set off interior Europe from its seaward margins. This zone became and has remained a disputed land—between Latin and Germanic culture in the west, and between Greek and Slavic culture in the east—with historical consequences of profound importance from that day to this.

North Central and Northeastern Europe remains dominantly Germanic and Slavic in blood, and until well into the Middle Ages these regions maintained their primordial life. In the coniferous forest the scattered tribesmen lived mainly by hunting. On the grassy plains nomadic bands roved with the cattle which provided their food, clothing, and habitations. Only step by step from west to east, did these modes of life give way to sedentary farming. In significant contrast, Northwest Europe became Romanized in language, customs, technology, and to some extent in blood. Later, the incursion of tribesmen from the east altered this provincial Roman society, but never wholly effaced the imprint of the Mediterranean world. For several centuries life in Northwest Europe was patterned as closely after Mediterranean Europe as its somewhat different natural environment would allow. Central Europe adopted Romanesque ways later, often at second hand, and always in dilute form.

LANDSCAPE PATTERNS

The Pattern of Mediterranean Europe

The basic Mediterranean design of living has always been small in scale (Fig. 5, p. 18). Each fertile lowland basin, such as Attica in Greece, Latium in Italy, and Carthagena in Spain, more or less cut off from its landward neighbors by rugged and unproductive hills or mountains, furnished a compact agricultural base for a small society. In periods such as the pre-classical and the medieval, when subsistence agriculture was the prime basis of life, each district could and did live mainly on its farm produce, supplemented along the coast by fish from the adjacent sea. At most seasons this inland sea is calm, and Mediterranean folk early took to fishing, in order to supplement the food supply of the restricted area that could be used for fields, orchards, and gardens.

From fishing to seaborne commerce is a natural step, and the farmers' and fishermen's market town, if it was situated at a focus of natural water routes and on a productive lowland and had a usable harbor, was likely to find itself a place of exchange for local and foreign goods. Towns with safe harbors, but not favored by nature in the other respects, were likely to engage in piracy, seizing goods that did not naturally flow to them. Opportunities for both legitimate and illicit trade proved less restricted than the resources of field and fishery, and thriving mercantile centers early dominated the life of the whole Mediterranean world, giving it an urban complexion it has never lost. Even in periods most inimical to trade, when prolonged warfare reduced transportation to the minimum, and cities found difficulty in feeding themselves, shrunken populations remained within town walls, and urban life survived. Vestiges of the city society of Classical Antiquity persisted everywhere in Mediterranean Europe throughout the Middle Ages, even though most of the staples of life had to be produced locally, and merchants who carried on the remnant trade were subjected to heavy taxes at home, and to peril of life when they ventured abroad.

In the course of history, small Mediterranean territorial units, each dominated by a town, have often been soldered together to form larger political units, their mutual foreign trade converted into domestic exchange, and their parallel lives enmeshed in a common net. Such political structures, after periods of expansion, have tended to break down, partly because of economic competition among their constituent units, based on similar natural resources. Even Rome, the most successful of Mediterranean empires, lost its cohesive power at last.

The prime characteristics of Mediterranean life sketched above have changed little throughout the course of history, apart from alternation between small states coterminous with local units of subsistence, and larger empires based on consolidation of local units.

One profound change in area occurred in the Middle Ages. In the seventh century the African shore of the Mediterranean Sea, and later the Asiatic shore, were overrun by Arabic civilization, and so lost to European culture. As part of Islam these large areas have never subsequently entered fully into European life, although gradually since the seventeenth century, section after section has been politically reconquered by European states and the whole area has tended to return to the European economic orbit. Throughout most of the Middle Ages it was known to Europeans only as the homeland of Moslem infidels, and a hostile land of deserts and semideserts. Occasionally chivalric crusading armies penetrated the boundary between Christian and Moslem, only to be decimated by the combined attrition of starvation, diseases rife in hot climates, and human enemies.

In the Mediterranean lands human life has fitted itself into a clear-cut environmental frame with remarkably little variation from age to age. Social customs and material technology that have been introduced from outside the region have likewise been molded to conform to the all-pervading pattern.

The Pattern of Northwest Europe

In Northwest Europe the natural environment is less decisive than in Mediterranean lands. It has permitted its inhabitants a wide latitude in making adaptations. The land was used rather differently in the classical and medieval periods, and between these earlier ages and the modern era the difference is even greater. Instead of shaping its inhabitants of whatever origin to a uniform pattern, it has permitted variety in economic use of the land and in contingent social structures.

The lowland units of Northwest Europe are larger, on the average, than those of the Mediterranean World (Fig. 5, p. 18). Commonly they are separated from each other by broad gentle hills, instead of being sharply cut off by rugged mountains. For example, if minor subdivisions are disregarded, all of lowland France falls into five major river basins; in contrast with peninsular Greece, where there are a dozen basins in an area less than one quarter as large. Moreover, the long coastline of the Mediterranean lands gives nearly every tiny lowland a seafront of its own, whereas in blockier Northwest Europe much of the land must gain access to the sea, if at all, by way of rivers or overland routes. Only on the Po Plain and the Iberian Plateau are size and access similar to conditions in the north. (It is significant that both these areas are also exceptions to the typical Mediterranean climate, being somewhat cut off from the equable sea (Fig. 4, p. 12).

Taking Northwest Europe as a whole, variety in both temperature and rainfall is greater than on the Mediterranean Sea borders. The range of latitude is wider, and the land extends inland some hundreds of miles, rather than a few dozen, and so partakes of the climatic conditions typical of continental interiors as well as of seacoasts.

In an area of such natural diversity, economic pursuits tend to be correspondingly varied and social groups are stamped with different character from place to place, even if they share a common origin. For example, coastal people devoted to fishing and seaborne trade incline to interest themselves in the larger world, whereas inlanders whose trade must be carried via costly land routes, or at best by rivers subject to interruption alternately by floods and low water, are likely to be more parochial in outlook.

Roman Impress on Northwest Europe. The Romans had been led to the naturally well-endowed northwestern part of the European continent by a desire to dominate the western basin of the Mediterranean Sea, their immediate goal being the Iberian Peninsula. The land route to Spain lay along the coast of southern France, a district of unalloyed Mediterranean character in climate, soils, and vegetation, and therefore easily assimilated by people from other Mediterranean shores. It was no accident that this coast became Rome's first province outside the Italian borders; hence its name *Provincia*, modern *Provence*. Once established there the Romans found it possible to control the Pyrenean passes, from a base in the broad gap between the Pyrenees and the *Massif Central*.

This *Massif* is formed by a block of low mountains. It occupies most of the Mediterranean hinterland between the Pyrenees and the Alps, but on each flank it leaves an open breach to the lowlands beyond. On the Pyrenean side an easy saddle leads to Aquitaine, the rich lowland of southwestern France, possessing a climate moister than that of the Mediterranean region, but not too different to be utilized by Roman settlers after some experimentation. Between the *Massif Central* and the Alps flows the Rhône River.

[29]

28918

That stream, with its tributary the Saône, leads by a water-level route to low passes connecting with both the Rhine and the Seine basins. This breach in the mountain wall is the sole direct and naturally-formed lowland line of access between the Mediterranean Sea and the heart of Northwest Europe. The Greeks had shown the way to it, planting a trading colony at Marseilles, on the natural harbor nearest the mouth of the Rhône. People bent on trade between the contrasting environments of north and south Europe have invariably followed this pathway in preference to any other. Whenever the conduct of the trade caused a struggle for political control, the same route proved to be the easiest line of march for armies.

The Romans took full advantage of the situation. They readily established themselves on the coastal lowland, so like their home-land in natural environment. They profited more slowly by its exceptional advantage—ready access to the north and west. First into Aquitaine, later up the Rhône, they thrust wedges of colo-nization so gradually that only by degrees did the intruding settlers find themselves in a non-Mediterranean environment.

In their slow progress inland they adapted their lives to novel elements in their new environment—colder winters, moist summers, thick deciduous forests, and large units of land. At the same time they brought into the northwest a technology that modified this environment. Wheat was adapted to the better-drained soils and to the less rainy lowlands in the lee of hills and mountains. The plow, rotation of crops, and the use of fertilizer were introduced. Mediterranean goods, including luxuries, were brought in, to be exchanged for forest products of the new lands, and later for farm products as well.

Towns grew up at route crossings to care for the trade—Lyons, Rheims, and London among many others. Along the frontier, com-bined trading and military posts were founded, such as Mainz and Cologne. Quickened economic life resulted from the application to novel environmental conditions of the Roman mode of state-craft. Roman legions succeeded in conquering the extensive plains and broad, intervening wooded heights of Northwest Europe, just as earlier they had conquered tiny Mediterranean lowlands sur-rounded by steep and narrow mountain ranges. Roman proconsuls then installed, with little modification, an administrative system which had operated successfully to unify the Mediterranean World. Perhaps the chief geographic contribution to Roman success was the system of paved roads which held the conquered terrain in a web, knotted the economic and political life of each section of lowland plain into an urban focus, and integrated the whole of Northwest Europe with the Mediterranean region by way of the Rhône breach and its less important alternate, the gap between the *Massif Central* and the Pyrenees.

Northwest Europe was susceptible to Romanization, not only because it was accessible from Rome's front dooryard, the Western Basin of the Mediterranean, but also because its natural environment was similar enough to permit easy adaptation of Mediterranean modes of life. Increasing distance from Rome and the corresponding contrast in environmental conditions inevitably left the farther regions less Romanized than the nearer areas. As a whole the Northwest appears to have lagged behind the Mediterranean region in effective utilization of its natural resources even during the epoch when Mediterranean technology was imposed upon it.

Roman Central Europe. Another territory conquered by Rome was less deeply etched with the Roman stamp. The belt of Alpine and Balkan mountains between Mediterranean and Central Europe was a naturally marked boundary zone, but when Rome occupied it, easy passes led to the annexation also of the hill lands between the mountains and the Danube River. Finally, the fertile plain north of the Danube's lower course was added, along with its encompassing low mountains. The utmost outpost of Roman authority in Europe, it was the last area to be incorporated into the Roman state and the first to be relinquished.

No other part of the Roman holdings was so unlike the Mediterranean environment as this strip of Danube country. Its summers are no hotter, but its winters are much colder. Fortunately the cold season is dry, and the rains fall in the summer growing season. Because the total precipitation is light, the natural vegetation was grassy, either with or without open woods, a kind of cover with which the Romans had learned to cope. Nevertheless, this southernmost belt of North Central Europe was not congenial to the Romans, and in the end the one obvious survival of their occupation was the language of Romania.

[31]

The Pattern of Central Europe

Under Roman dominion the Mediterranean World and Northwest Europe worked out a reasonably unified, harmonious life, despite differences of natural environment. In sharp contrast, no attempt was ever made to imprint the landscape design normal to Mediterranean coastlands upon the country beyond the boundary of the Roman Empire. As a consequence, the differences springing from natural contrasts were accentuated by modes of living at variance with each other. This was probably inevitable where the broad and lofty mountains of Central Europe set the tiny, warm, dry, and fertile coastlands of the south definitively apart from the large, rainy, infertile, inland plains of the north. The transitional belt between Alps-Balkans and Danube was too narrow to act as an effective bridge between the strongly contrasted Roman and "barbarian" societies (Fig. 4, p. 12).

The Rhine below its Great Elbow (at Basel), is a less obvious barrier. Within that part of the Rhine Basin no striking contrast occurs in natural conditions, and the ranges of low mountains west of the stream are breached at numerous points. The river lies in a zone of transition in respect to land-relief, climate, soil, and natural vegetation. Yet neither the stream itself, its valley walls, nor its watershed, constitute an environmental barrier between Northwest and Central Europe. Throughout most of its basin, favored districts yield satisfactory harvests of Mediterranean wheat and grapes. In accessibility also, the Rhineland is similar to Northwest rather than to Central Europe. Connections with the sea are alike in Western Germany and Eastern France. From the vicinity of the Great Elbow, a broad gap between the Jura and the Vosges mountains links the Rhine Valley to the Mediterranean Sea by way of the Rhône Valley.

The transitional Rhineland might have served as a link between Central Europe and Northwest Europe, but the nature of each of the flanking regions has remained distinct. East of a line connecting the Danish Peninsula with the west end of the Bohemian mountains, the contrast with Northwest Europe becomes strongly marked (Fig. 5, p. 18). The landscape flattens and broadens. Mountain ranges are few and low, many of them being named "forests," rather than "mountains." Lowland units are large and monotonously uniform. There is no contact with the ocean except by way of the Baltic Sea, and its shoreline is short in ratio to the tributary land area. Moreover, its harbors are few and shallow, and its entrance is subject to control by the people who occupy its narrow outlet. Rivers lie far apart, several of them flow in parallel courses instead of diverging from a common center as in Northwest Europe, and all of them empty into enclosed seas. They are further reduced in utility by being ice-blocked nearly half the year. The cold and snowy winters that lock the streams confine the growth of crops to a short season. The summers, in spite of brief hot spells, are so cool and rainy everywhere north of Hungary that staple foods are restricted to the less desirable crops—barley, oats, rye, and buckwheat. Considerable acreages cannot support even these, because, overlaid with sterile sand and in the natural state covered with forest or with useless heath, they are fitted at best to grow pine trees. Other extensive areas are dotted with lakes and marshes, or crisscrossed with wet swales and river floodplains. These features, like the sandy soils, are earmarks of the glacial epoch. So long as this area lay beyond the Roman frontier, it remained a land sparsely peopled with tribesmen of the forest who lived mainly by the chase. Tillage of the soil was a secondary business to a people moving about in pursuit of game. Towns did not exist. For three or more centuries the Rhine River was maintained as a military and cultural boundary, and marked a line in the transition zone that accentuated the separation of two contrasted types of landscape and two equally distinct modes of settlement.

Medieval Modifications of the Landscape Pattern

When the Roman military defense weakened, Germanic tribesmen from beyond the Rhine-Danube boundary broke into the Empire along its whole length. As these incursions grew to the proportions of folk migrations, they broke down the Roman mode of life. True, the stream of migrating folk that poured across the disrupted frontier became increasingly diluted with local blood as it penetrated ever more deeply into the Romanized world. Nevertheless, nearly the whole area lapsed into an economy largely rural and able to produce little beyond the minimum requirements of subsistence for the population. This backward condition lasted throughout the centuries when the chaotic and localized rule of the early Middle Ages replaced the ordered, centralized government of Rome.

Central Europe. The first territories lost to Rome were by location and environment parts of Central Europe. All the districts beyond the Danube and the Rhine were either incompletely conquered or tenuously held, and they were overrun a century or more before the river boundaries gave way. After removing the capital to Constantinople, the (East) Roman Empire had a military base which enabled its rulers to hold the line of the Lower Danube until long after the entire western Roman world had dissolved into Germanic Kingdoms. When finally the imperial boundary in the east was retracted from the Danube River to the Balkan Mountains, it remained impregnable to attacks from the north.

The first effective penetration of the river frontiers occurred at about the turn of the fifth century. Germanic tribes crossed the Middle Danube and, a few years later, the Upper Rhine. These moves heralded widespread incursions into Western Europe. It is not surprising that the part of the Empire belonging physically to Central Europe should have proved the weak spot in the imperial armor when probed by Central Europeans.

Northwest Europe. Once the river frontiers had given way, Germanic tribes flooded the western Roman World. The incursions did not follow an orderly pattern, but the most exposed parts suffered first and were altered the most.

Remote and insular Britain was on the extreme frontier of the Empire after the capital was removed to Constantinople, whereas it lay close to the Germanic tribes along the North Sea coast of continental Europe. As the Rhine-Danube frontier was being crossed by wandering landsmen, sea rovers traversed the "narrow seas" to the British Isles. To strengthen the defenses of Rome, the legions were withdrawn from Britain, leaving the way clear for a folk-migration in the wake of piratical forays.

Continental Northwest Europe was inundated by the tide of folk movements along the entire Rhine frontier. Germanic settlements were made early in the Rhône and Garonne basins, later in the Seine lowland, but all within the fifth century. The whole area was vulnerable to incursions by these hordes of forest dwellers because it lacked the protection of lofty, forested, barrier mountains (Figs. 2, p. 6, and 5, p. 18). There also it proved difficult to

[34]

reconstitute stable government after the folk-migrations came to a halt. This may have been due in part to the relatively short period of Roman rule in the region. It seems to have been related also to the character of the country.

Much of its large, productive, lowland area either lay inland or faced a turbulent ocean. Few, if any, of the small political units were set off from envious neighbors by any natural barriers more effective than wooded hills or belts of marsh, and all of them were exposed to enemies at several points. It was therefore difficult for the inhabitants to protect themselves against invasion with accompanying destruction of capital goods—of everything, in fact, except the land itself.

In a warlike age the most reliable source of livelihood is farming, because armies rarely put the land permanently out of use. Nevertheless, they consume or destroy the crops and livestock. Medieval farming, subjected as it was to repeated depredations, and lacking the benefit of exchanging products among diverse regions, long remained at a low level that barely sufficed to yield subsistence. The rather sparse population lived mainly on the soil and operated a farming system surprisingly uniform for so varied an area.

Everywhere pastures, while most productive in summer, remained green throughout the cool winter, thus providing feed for animals throughout the year. Staple crops invariably included wheat, an immigrant from the Mediterranean region, and prized since Roman times as the staff of life. In the wetter climates, on heavy soils, and in highlands, it yielded very poor returns. The other staple crops—oats, barley, buckwheat, and rye—were considered inferior, but were widely grown, especially on the less fertile lands, because of their greater hardiness in comparison to wheat, and correspondingly higher yields. Very slowly, as population increased and government became effective in ever larger units, subsistence agriculture gave place to specialization in crops and livestock adapted to the rich and diverse lowlands of Northwest Europe, and to exchange-economy based on such specialization.

Both trade and crafts are highly vulnerable to war and the threat of war, and consequently trading and handicraft towns came into existence only toward the end of the medieval period. When they did take their rise, they appeared first along the seacoast and

FIG. 6. MEDIEVAL TRADE ROUTES

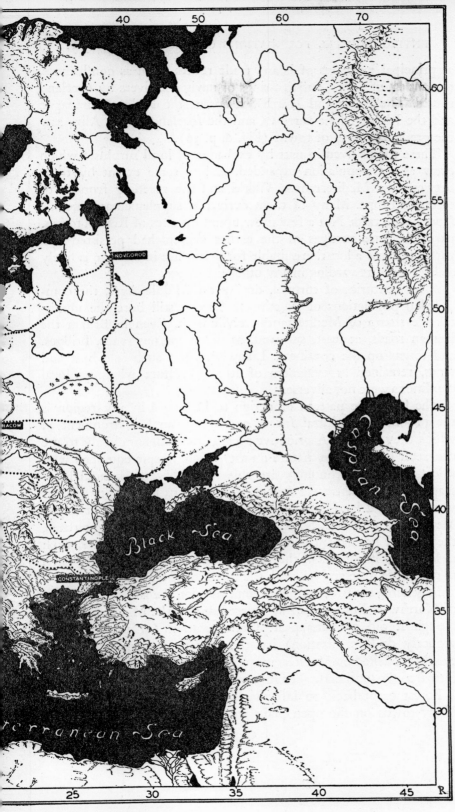

AND TRADING CITIES.

at principal junctions of inland trade routes, such as confluences, the outlets of passes, and crossings of navigable rivers by overland routes. The Baltic and North Sea coasts, the Rhône-Champagne and the Rhône-Rhine furrows, and the foreland of the Alps, saw the gradual growth of towns (Fig. 6, p. 36).

These towns lived in part by exchange of local surpluses which grew as the population expanded, and to some extent by trade between the Mediterranean World and the receding frontier of eastern Europe. Many of them derived a supplementary income from handicrafts. Not a few grew up on the sites of Roman towns, partly because vestiges of the earlier centers had persisted and partly because a location suitable for urban life in one age is likely to be equally rewarding in any other urban age.

After centuries of turmoil, during the Middle Ages, the commingled populations of Northwest Europe still bore the unmistakable stamp of Mediterranean civilization. Even in Britain the Roman roads, at least, survived, as did numerous roads, bridges, and towns on the continent. Likewise crops, such as wheat and vines, remained as evidences of Roman culture wherever local conditions were not adverse.

The landscape pattern or design to be found in any region is the product of cultural forces and the natural environment in which they operate. A primitive society must adhere closely to the character bestowed by nature on the region. People equipped with a less primitive technology are able to modify the natural landscape to a commensurate degree. The Romans brought to Northwest Europe a landscape design that had been worked out in the Mediterranean world. Some elements of it, such as straight roads, they added permanently to the northern landscape; others, such as life lived in the open, they failed to establish; still others, such as urban life, rose and fell with the fortunes of Rome.

In general, the Mediterranean imprint upon the landscape pattern of Northwest Europe became blurred during the Middle Ages, although it did not disappear. Germanization (or perhaps more properly de-Romanization) led the way to a mode of life less closely modelled on Mediterranean practices, and more neatly conformal to the local natural environment.

Forest crept back on infertile land no longer used for fields. Many towns on the open plain were deserted for safer sites on hills or islands, and detours from the straight Roman roads led to these new defense points. Streams once again had to bear the bulk of commerce, and towns and castles became oriented to the lines of waterways. In short, the natural character of Northwest Europe reappeared as the Mediterranean veneer cracked and chipped, and was partially replaced by Germanic inlay. The resultant landscape was neither Roman nor German, but a composite in which the usages and the technology of both were adapted to the local natural environment.

Mediterranean Europe. Within the basin of the Western Mediterranean the Roman way of life was less markedly affected than in the north. The Roman stamp was that of Mediterranean culture, and it had the resilience of a society harmoniously interwoven with its natural environment. Besides, the Germanic impress was much lighter than in North Europe. Fewer invaders reached so far from their homelands, each group that did so was cut off from contact with its previous habitat in the North European forest, and the distinctive Mediterranean environment was too unlike the northern forest country to be readily altered.

Changes observable in the landscape were associated with weakening and splitting of governmental units. Economic ties between regions were cut or frayed, so that trade was reduced and subsistence agriculture increased at the expense of commercial specialization. Large-scale irrigation works fell into disuse as population declined. Erosion of denuded hills carried fertile soil off the farms, while deposition filled navigable streams with silt, and turned tidal flats into malarial marshes. Many lowland market towns were deserted in favor of hamlets perched on easily defended hills.

THE ENVIRONMENTAL BASE OF MEDIEVAL SOCIETY

Blurring of the Boundaries

The political hand of Rome has lain heavy upon Europe for two thousand years. Nevertheless, its weight should not be overestimated. So long as the political boundary of the Roman Empire was maintained at a fixed line, such as the Rhine or the Danube River, outpost trading towns flourished on frontier trade with the Germanic and Slavic peoples beyond the boundary. When the political frontier was retracted, transition zones were left as districts once

Roman but now again outside the Empire. Many of their inhabitants fled to take refuge behind the retreating frontier. Others must have stayed and intermingled with the incoming tribesmen, creating a new society of combined Roman and German elements. During the period of Roman decline, increasing numbers of "barbarians" obtained permission to settle within the confines of the Empire.

The Empire by slow stages disintegrated as a political entity, and ultimately lay wide open to immigrants from Central Europe. At the same time, the people who remained in Central Europe were busily identifying their civilization with that of the Roman World. The lands both within and without the former Empire were reconstituted into political units of varying size and fluctuating boundaries, diverse in their political character from place to place, and from generation to generation.

Most of them fell into a simple landscape design in which mode of life was intimately related to natural conditions while superimposed cultural distinctions faded. Hence, the design differed in detail from place to place with varying combinations of the elements constituting the natural environment. In essentials it was remarkably uniform, both in the Roman world and in Central, non-Romanized Europe.

With the relaxation of Rome's political sway in the fourth and fifth centuries, the ordered economic society of the Empire gave way to confusion. Trade dwindled, and Europeans were increasingly thrown back upon local resources for their livelihood. This inevitably meant a reduction in the variety of goods available for people of every class, because no small area can produce as varied products as can the whole earth, or even such a considerable part of the earth as the Romans had incorporated in their Empire.

Many goods formerly abundant could no longer be obtained at any price. Only the very wealthy could pay the high cost of bringing goods from afar, and thereby benefit from using the contrasted resources of different regions. Barring a very few necessities, such as iron and copper for utensils and implements, and salt, the common man had to be content with what could be produced on land within a day's walk of his home. Towns shrank or even disappeared, as townsfolk lost their chief businesses—trade, and such crafts as contributed to trade. Food was easily available only in the countryside; consequently the European populace during the Middle Ages was organized primarily as a rural society. The few surviving urban centers were chiefly market towns, engaged in weekly exchange of the products of a small district, or holding occasional fairs to which itinerant merchants brought wares from a distance, for a day, a week, or a month.

Geography of the Manor

The basic unit in rural medieval society was the manor. The manor should not be thought of as narrowly administrative in character, for it also had a geographic aspect as a unit of land.

Both before and after the political disintegration of the western Roman Empire, say from the third to the tenth centuries (the so-called Dark Ages), population decreased. The total amount of land devoted to farming diminished to correspond with the reduced demand for food. The fields selected to be kept under the plow were those that would yield a fair crop with the least labor, because the shrinkage of population reduced available field hands as well as consuming mouths. The land not needed for cultivation was allowed to revert to a state of nature. This varied in character with climate, landforms, and soils.

In the Mediterranean lowlands irrigation canals generally silted up or were choked by weeds, and the land they had served was perforce abandoned or planted only to winter crops. Drainage ditches likewise became clogged, with the result that flat lands such as coastal plains, river floodplains, and deltas, relapsed into marsh. Carefully made walls supporting farmed terraces on the hillsides broke down for lack of labor to repair them, and these old fields, along with the hilly and mountainous lands generally, grew up to a tangle of brush, producing nothing more than a little forage for sheep and goats.

In Northwest Europe farming practice had never been so intensive as in the South. There, abandonment of fields was generally followed by the resurgence of forest. In a surprisingly short time the tilled patches lay scattered through a matrix of woodland —a source of game, lumber, firewood, and a few nuts, but far less productive than the fields it replaced. Pigs could and did wrest a living from the mast of the forests. Woods closely encompassed the patches of open land, and so could be used as an adjunct of the farm property. Except for the predominance of deciduous trees rather than conifers, the region presumably came to look not unlike Central Europe, a region that had never been subject to the farm practices instituted by the Romans, and hence had not been denuded of its forest cover.

In Central Europe the roving Germanic and Slavic peoples made closer contacts with the Romanized world after the political boundary of the Empire disappeared. As they settled themselves in fixed habitations and made tillage of the soil their primary business, clearings increased in number and size.

Layout of the Manor. The manor was the basic unit of land, and evolved from Roman practice and custom, especially in those parts of Europe north of the mountains, but also in many Mediterranean areas. It consisted of a nucleus of arable land, surrounded by pasture and woodland. Its boundaries ran mostly through forests in the north, and across scrub-covered hills in the south.

The settlement stood convenient to water—a spring or brook, or a place where a shallow well could tap an underground supply. On a choice site rose the manor house, residence of the family which held title to the property. Where the terrain permitted, the site of the house took advantage of natural defense, such as a hill or a cliff, a stream or lake. In especially troublous times or in exposed locations, the manor-house was fortified by a wall, constructed so as to aid the men of the community in its defense. Close by was the church with the rectory.

A little farther off, the farm village straggled along both sides of a road, perhaps the only connection the manor had with the outside world. Each farm family occupied a cottage, frequently under the same roof as the stable and barn. The farmyard, haystacks, and kitchen garden were close to the house. Beyond, and scattered from one end to the other of the manorial plowland, lay the many plots which together comprised the fields of each farmer.

The number of families in the village was determined by the amount of arable land available. The theoretical upper limit was an acreage so large that to reach the more remote fields and pastures entailed a walk of a couple of hours. Generally the limit was more narrowly fixed by nature—a valley lowland sharply bounded by hills, a plain between marshy streams, a fertile stretch of land surrounded by relatively unproductive soils. Whatever the limitation, the arable tract had to be large relative to the population of the manor, because the system of land-holding and crop production held even the most fertile soils down to low output.

In a region of such diversity of landforms and climate as Europe, soils are certain to vary greatly. Those of sandy areas, common in North Central Europe, contained little plant food to begin with, and were soon depleted. Their one virtue was ready drainage, a real asset in the rainy, cool climate of this region. Heavy silts and clays, found on river floodplains and deltas, and overlying shales and some limestones, were cultivable in the dry Mediterranean region, but in the rainier north were generally left in pasture. The soils most highly prized everywhere were found on limestone plains. These soils retained their productivity longer than the light soils and were adequately drained and at the same time retentive of sufficient moisture to guard against dry spells.

Even the most fertile soil must be well treated, if it is to maintain its productivity. After the decline of the relatively advanced Roman farming practices, there was scarcely any manure available on the manor for fertilizing the fields, because the livestock grazed at large, and of course chemical fertilizers were unknown. Therefore it was necessary for the land to rest frequently, so that nature might have an opportunity to rid it of toxic substances and to replenish a measure of the natural plant foods withdrawn by the crops.

The Fields and the Crops. In the early Middle Ages only half the arable land was tilled each year, the other half being left fallow. Later on, farm practice improved, and it became the rule to plant the land for two consecutive years, leaving it fallow during the third. This is the so-called "three-field system" of agriculture. It was finally abandoned in France only at the time of the 18th-century Revolution, in Russia with the Bolshevik Revolution of 1917 and the years following, and not even yet in out-of-the-way corners of East Central Europe.

In order to give each farmer a fair share of all available types of soil, drainage, and exposure to sun and wind, the arable land was divided into many strips, the number being determined by the local diversity of landforms and soils.

The shape of each piece of land was a long, narrow rectangle. It had to be long to facilitate plowing. The crude, wooden or iron-shod plow was about the only piece of farm machinery in common use. The suitable length for a furrow (a furrow long, or furlong) was generally accepted as ⅛ of a mile or 40 rods. So long a strip had to be narrow in order to give every farmer a fair share of each sort of land. It was ordinarily about a rod (16½ feet) wide.

It was manifestly impracticable to allow every farmer to decide which of his tiny strips to leave fallow, and what crops to plant on the remainder. Therefore some accepted authority divided the total arable land of the manor into three great sections of equal area, taking care to equalize the various kinds of land in each third. These constituted the "three fields," and in turn each was (1) planted to wheat (rye in the cold northeast and on infertile soils elsewhere), (2) then to a variety of less desired crops, such as oats, barley, and buckwheat, and (3) finally left fallow. Each farmer was compelled to plant or fallow his strips as they fell into one or the other of the three fields. Thus in any one year, one-third of the land was planted to bread food for the inhabitants of the manor, and one-third to stock-feed, grain for the local alcoholic drink, and minor human foods. The remainder, while lying fallow, could be used for grazing stock, and it thus got a little manuring, but not enough to do much good.

Crops requiring less land, such as garden vegetables, olives, wine, nuts, and fruits, were grown in the manorial garden and orchard for the benefit of the lord and his family, and in the kitchen yards of the farmers.

The Livestock. The manorial field crops produced for livestock only grain feed, and none too much of that. Poultry scratched about the village and in the fields to pick up what living it could. Stubblefields and fallow lands provided poor pickings at some seasons for grazing-animals, but the stock had to live chiefly on pasturage. In the south, sheep and goats nibbled the brush of the hills, and a few cattle could subsist on the scattered marshy lowlands; in summer the hillside forage ran very short. In the north cattle predominated over sheep, and both grazed the manorial pasturage adjacent to the fields. Generally pasturage was relegated to hill land, wet valley floor, heavy soil, thin soil on porous ridges, or infertile heath. In summer both cattle and sheep fared well on these lands, but in winter, especially in the more extreme climate of Central Europe, the animals lost weight.

[44]

At the end of the lean season the scrawny stock was far from fit. This was serious in the case of draft animals. Half-starved, the oxen or cows commonly used were too weak to pull the plow if it was thrust deep into the soil. The inevitable shallow plowing left the land ill-prepared, and its yield was light, even in favorable seasons. Fortunately, wheat was fall-sown, and preparation of the wheat fields found the animals in better condition. But at best the ox-yoke and the medieval plow were inefficient contrivances, although they were the only mechanical devices used by many generations of farmers.

Output improved when the collar for horse or ass was substituted for the ox-yoke. The farmers who could afford to adopt the improvement could plow more deeply and in normal years accumulated a surplus of agricultural products. Yokes of oxen continued in general use, however, because these beasts were cheaper than horses or mules.

The Common Lands. The pastureland was used in common by all the farmers, and was not fenced. Boys, men, or women were delegated to keep the stock off the fields, and to prevent their straying into the woodland.

The surrounding forest or brush was by no means useless. It afforded feed for pigs, chiefly in the north but also in the oak forests of the Iberian Peninsula. Members of the community gleaned twigs for firewood or charcoal, and in the off-season, cut trees for buildings or fences. Ordinarily the forest, like the village mill for grinding grain and the huge oven for baking bread, was used in common, but owned by the lord of the manor, who charged the farm families in kind for the use they made of all these facilities.

At best the manorial farm system used the land wastefully, and one of the most fundamental and far-reaching differences between medieval and modern times is the increased efficiency in utilizing the greatest of all natural resources, the soil, characteristic of European agriculture in recent centuries.

The Growth of Land Units

The manor was primarily a unit of farmland. It was too uniform to provide economic diversity, and too small to support a political organization of any consequence. It may be thought of as the cell-unit of medieval agricultural society. The combining of several manorial cells resulted in the creation of organs of that society—entities which retained their rural character while taking on political functions. Agglomeration of diverse lands and their inhabitants provided a broad enough economic base to sustain a political structure and might constitute an incipient state. If it was sufficiently favored by nature and by vigorous and successful policy on the part of its rulers, it grew by accretion. The more successful of these political entities were kernels of political units that make up the modern European world.

During all the earlier Middle Ages, however, territorial disintegration prevailed over integration, until finally the ancient tradition of the Roman Empire became an empty form, without power beyond the force which the current emperor derived from his personal landholdings. The territory which slipped from the imperial grasp fell, in blocks of varying size, into the hands of rulers who inherited political functions commensurate with their holdings. These ranged from kingship down to presiding over petty neighborhood courts.

The least of the administrators owned, operated, and gained his living from a single manor. Others had several. More often than not the manors belonging to any one lord were scattered about among holdings of other and often rival landowners. The larger landlords came to have two sorts of holdings: the demesne, consisting of the manors held directly and relied upon for the livelihood of the owner and his administrative officers; and lands granted in some sort of fee to other lords, as a rule in return for military service.

Any number of elements entered into the successful construction of a state out of the manorial building cells. The energy and shrewdness of the ruler played a part, and no doubt luck figured in many cases. Nevertheless, some holdings possessed environmental advantages over others. These, being continuously in force from century to century, worked for political superiority or supremacy in the long run.

Farmlands. In a rural age the chief value of the land was inevitably its fitness for agriculture. Fertile and well-drained soil was the only sort that could be profitably tilled by the sparse, poor population of the earlier Middle Ages. Suitable land was likely to be found on lowland plains facing the sea, in segments of river valleys, on well drained plains between streams, abutting marshy floodplains, and in fertile spots amid forested sand plains. In such localities people could make an assured living and in the course of generations win something more than subsistence, thus fitting themselves to take part in the complex life of farms, trades, and crafts that developed during the later Middle Ages.

In that era of perennial fighting, when any petty ruler might be ranged against his neighbor, a lord who could push the boundaries of his holdings to some natural barrier had a military advantage over one whose arbitrary bounds were marked only by agreement. Barrier boundaries commonly found in medieval Europe were broad marshes, impassible gorges in river valleys, wastes of heath or scrub, forbidding, dense forests, and less commonly, mountain ranges.

The successive concentric ranges of hills which surround Paris (Fig. 5, p. 18), particularly well-developed on the east and almost reaching the Rhine River, appear to have been an important factor in the establishment of Paris and its surrounding territory as the core of the French state. On a smaller scale, the Dutch nation owes its distinctiveness in part to barrier-marshes among which it took shape. Dozens of other small regions have had their political heyday, only to disappear when their protective barriers were destroyed, as by felling forests or draining marshes, or when they were reduced in potency by improved technology, as by building engineered roads through mountain passes.

Protecting barriers were important to a budding state, but no more so than an easily defended site so located as to serve readily as the focus of life for the whole unit. Perhaps the most prized site for defense was the crest of an isolated, cliff-sided hill where drinking water could be had from a spring or shallow well. A flat-top was useful, but not required, and further protection might be lent by stream washing the base of the cliff. Lacking an isolated eminence, the end of a spur might be utilized by walling it off. In flat country, islands in streams or lakes were commonly utilized. Sometimes an island was created by an artificial moat, particularly if this could be done merely by diverting part of a stream.

Trade Centers. However well defended by nature, a political unit lacked an essential quality if it was separated from the life-giving currents of human movement. Trade never wholly ceased

[47]

in the darkest age, and as time passed it consistently grew (Fig. 6, p. 36). Some of the most strongly fortified political centers of the period were on trade routes, located so as to protect the traffic or to levy toll upon it. A narrows on a navigable river, across which a chain might be stretched as a toll-gate, was a favored site. The mouth of a mountain pass was an obvious bottleneck, easily controlled. Trade was redoubled at a crossing of routes, especially if no alternate competitive route intersection could be found, as at a confluence of waterways. A point where an overland route traversed a navigable stream favored exchange. Except in flat country the exact site of such a crossing was usually determined by the convergence of tributary valleys from opposite sides of the stream. Wherever it was necessary or desirable to shift from one mode of transportation to another, a center might grow up. The head of an estuary on a coastal lowland requires transfer from ocean ships to river craft, and may also be the point farthest down-stream easily bridged to facilitate overland trade. Along the base of every mountain range are centers which have thriven on the change in mode of transportation between mountain trails and plains roads.

In many instances unrivalled value of a site for trade caused a commercial town to be chosen as a political capital, even if nature provided no aids for its defense. Often the chief manor house of a nobleman was the focus of life for the people of his territory, whether the protection afforded was based on nature or created by man. Thither the farmer folk went to hold their weekly market, to settle their grievances under the lord's arbitration, and to make carnival.

The prosperity of such a center kept pace with the expansion of the lord's agricultural lands and his opportunities to tap trade and to foster handicrafts. One of the principal achievements of the Middle Ages turned out to be the amalgamation of manorial cell-units into firmly knit and interdependent statelets that became increasingly prosperous.

Quarries and Mines. Some budding political units profited from possession of minerals valuable to the simple society of the Middle Ages. Since minerals lay buried and scattered in no discernable relation to surface features of the earth, discovery of their existence often proved an unexpected source of wealth for the lord of the land. Mining settlements added themselves to the other towns of the region, and miners became a category of specialized laborers who moved about from one center to another as new mines were opened. The list of minerals valued in medieval times was short (Fig. 7, p. 50). Salt was always in demand both for seasoning and preserving food. Copper and tin were still used for bronze, but iron was fast supplanting the alloy for tools and weapons. Copper and lead were in demand for roofing, and lead for setting glass windows. Gold and silver were then as now valued for ornaments and as evidence of wealth. Coal was known but its utility was not. Glass sand of high quality was the basis of a localized handicraft. Building minerals—stone, sand, clay, and lime—were too heavy to ship far. The variation in architecture from locality to locality which still gives Europe much of its charming variety began to take shape from medieval use of local building materials. Aside from important structures, there was a striking contrast between the stone and plaster construction in the wood-poor Mediterranean region, and frame and half-timbered buildings in the forested north. Even churches, town halls, and manor houses, built for permanence and hence with a minimum of wood, varied from limestone or sandstone and slate, where they outcropped, to brick and tile where the solid rock was deeply buried beneath unconsolidated sediments, as on river deltas, or where the underlying rocks were unsuited for building-stone.

VARIETY AND UNITY

Variety is the keynote of the European environment. No other continent possesses an equal area with so wide a range of habitats well suited to human occupance. They run the gamut from vast to tiny. For example, the entire Mediterranean basin is in considerable degree unified by a distinctive climate and innumerable small valleys facing the sea and backed by mountains. But within that basin are subdivisions as different as the dry, rugged, and bare Aegean islets, the broad, lush Po Plain with its flat deltaic coast, and the semi-arid Spanish plateau, cut off from the sea by mountain ranges. An equal diversity can be found in both the other broad divisions of the continent—the Northwest and the North Center.

Medieval society in each of the three principal parts inherited a distinctive mode of life which reinforced the major natural contrasts. The breakdown of transport for goods and of security for

MEDIEVAL
MINERAL RESOURCES

SCALE OF MILES

0   100   200   400   600

CONIC PROJECTION

Fig. 7. MEDIEVAL

MINERAL RESOURCES.

the traveller kept people and their wares close to home and so aided further subdivision. The lesser units were likely to correspond roughly with bounds of natural features—landforms, soil, vegetation, or local climate.

Not all the trends were divisive. Forces for unity coexisted with the tendency to fall apart. The ideal of world (*i. e.* European) unity was preserved with varying success—less in the political realm and more in the ecclesiastical sphere—but diminishing in both. Regional unification on a scale less than continental was fostered by the very diversity of earth conditions. Adjacent regions having contrasting products of field, forest, mine, or sea to exchange could facilitate a pooling of resources by political union. All the larger states of modern Europe have thus consolidated contrasting regions, with commensurate strengthening of their economic base and political force. This trend began with the Middle Ages.

CHAPTER III

Europe on the Threshold of the Discoveries

In terms of the earth and its utilization, the business of the Middle Ages turned out to be fourfold: (1) to regain for agriculture some or all of the land lost to use in the break-up of classical civilization, and to add to the total land in farms a vast acreage north and east of the old Roman Empire; (2) to discover new sources of mineral wealth, and to amplify both the number of minerals used and ways of using them; (3) to reëstablish intercourse between isolated regions, and to increase the exchange of products and ideas between areas made reciprocal by contrasting natural endowment; and (4) to consolidate political society into blocks larger and economically more coherent than the random and fragmentary groupings of self-subsistent manorial cell-units of the Dark Ages.

EUROPEAN EXPANSION EASTWARD

Some progress in all these respects was unceasing, even during the centuries of greatest retrogression. But at first the forces of disintegration were superior to those of integration. In the geographic sense, the Middle Ages began to give way to the Modern Period when Europe, having set its house in order, generated enough force to expand beyond its traditional boundaries both on land and by sea. By the tenth century the seeds of this expansion had been sown, and during the subsequent fivehundred years modern Western Society was germinating (Fig. 1c, p. 2).

The Armed Frontier

The first stirrings of expansion were tentative and took the form of sporadic border fighting along the eastern frontier of medieval Europe. This thrust eastward was essentially similar to the much later push of white settlers westward in North America. The inhabitants of eastern Europe were either nomadic horsemen of the grassy plains or less mobile but nevertheless migrant tribes of the forest (Fig. 2, p. 6). They were heathen in an age aflame with the missionary spirit of Christianity, and like unsettled peoples everywhere, they made repeated incursions across the boundary and devastated sedentary Christian settlements that lived by growing crops in the European tradition. The strong contrast in mode of life and in ideals laid the foundation for a life-and-death struggle, for which depredations all along the frontier furnished ample provocation to both sides.

During the earlier Middle Ages the eastern frontier of Europe lay for centuries in what is now central Germany. It took advantage of natural barriers—marsh and heath in the north, and forested ridges or hill lands between the flat coastal plain and the eastern Alps Mountains. Thence it followed the northern frontier of the Byzantine (Roman) Empire along the Balkans and into Asia Minor. Slowly and intermittently the expansive force from the west pushed the frontier eastward. Europeans flowed down the narrow Danube Valley into the Middle Basin of that stream, and, more slowly, spread out along the Baltic on the broad northern plain. They did not succeed in dislodging the Slavs who were settled behind the rugged ranges, called by several names, which lay between the two lowland passageways (Fig. 5, p. 18). As the thrust eastward continued it met increasing resistance all along the line. Central Asiatic horsemen under Mongol direction drove across the Urals and around their southern end. On the plain far to the west of this range they halted the advancing Europeans. As late as the opening of the fifteenth century, these Mongol tribes reached their maximum territorial extension—a line not far east of the Vistula River (Fig. 6, p. 36).

At the same period the Turks—like the Mongols, originally

nomads from interior Asia—were making their way from Asia Minor into the Danube country. After signalizing their enduring establishment in Europe by taking Constantinople, the capital of Byzantine Rome, they crossed the Balkan Peninsula and moved up the Danube. They exhausted their thrust before the gates of Vienna, but not until almost two centuries after the Mongols had disappeared as a power on the plains of the north.

These forays into Europe by nomadic Asiatics may have been caused by a prolonged period of drouth and suffering in their semi-arid homeland. The eastward expansion of Europeans north of the Alps, with its frontier turbulence, certainly followed upon an upturn in population growth in sedentary Europe during the Middle Ages, and the consequent land hunger. During the same period Europeans were expending some of their accumulated energy in commercial ventures in the eastern basin of the Mediterranean Sea.

Commercial Stirrings

From a low point during the barbarian invasions, trade slowly increased in volume and in radius. Within Europe some of this movement of goods arose from differences in economic level— between the frontier and the older settlements, and between the south (where the Roman economic structure had been less completely destroyed than in the north) and the more Germanized areas (Fig. 5, p. 18). Some trade sprang from permanent environmental differences, such as localization of minerals, and particularly the contrast in climate between Mediterranean and North Europe. These mainsprings of commerce, economic and environmental, likewise stimulated exchange between Europe as a whole and the world beyond the desert enclosing the coastlands at the eastern end of the Mediterranean Sea (Fig. 2, p. 6). Central, South, and East Asia were not known to Europeans by direct contact, but the luxury goods produced there—silks, woven rugs, lacquer, jewels, and carved ivory and jade—were highly prized, while their pepper and spices were necessities in an age of monotonous and unrefrigerated food. A few Mediterranean towns had always participated in this trade as middlemen, and others joined in as the business grew with the general rise in the level of European prosperity.

[55]

Crusading Movements. It so happened that the increasing demand for Asiatic goods synchronized with the westward thrust of nomads from interior Asia, both on the North European Plain and in the Danube Basin and the Balkans. Before the Turks invaded Europe, they had pushed overland in successive waves to the eastern end of the Mediterranean Sea. Being Moslems, these new-comers were in the position of heretical conquerors and infidel occupants of Palestine, the Holy Land of Christian Europe. This spurred the missionary spirit, which had already been partly re-sponsible for drives against heathen on the northeastern frontier and Moslems in Iberia. In 1089 all Europe was set aflame when the first crusade against the infidels in Palestine was preached. For the next two hundred years crusading armies were sent to West Asia at intervals of a generation or so, and scarcely a season passed without some movement of fighting men thither. The first drive was moderately successful, and feudal states were set up in the Asiatic lands wrested from the Moslems. It is pertinent to note that the most powerful and enduring of these states were not in Pales-tine, a niggardly land, but farther north, at the end of the ancient overland trade route between Mesopotamia (the Tigris-Euphrates lowland) and the Mediterranean Sea—the route that had nourished the Phoenicians, their Greek successors, and Roman Antioch (Fig. 3, p. 10).

Successive crusading expeditions, supported chiefly by north Europeans, added to the wealth of the Mediterranean cities, and powerfully stimulated the purchase of Asiatic goods everywhere in Europe. Incidentally, they awakened a Europe-wide interest in the Mediterranean World that bore fruit in a revival of classical learning and contributed ultimately to the Renaissance and the era of modern thought.

As a military venture against the infidel, each Crusade after the first failed more lamentably than its predecessor. The ensuing counter-thrust from the dry core of Asia was too vigorous to over-come, and one by one the Christian states in the Eastern Medi-terranean were reconquered by Turkish armies. During the fourteenth and fifteenth centuries, the European expansive effort found itself blocked in its traditional, eastward, overland movement all the way from the Arctic Ocean to the Arabian desert. The nascent oriental sea trade was killed almost at birth. The expansive force of Europe was thereupon turned to exploring the seaways of the "Western Ocean."

EUROPEAN EXPANSION OVERSEAS

The goal of all the seagoing explorations launched by Europeans at the end of the Middle Ages was Asia (Fig. 2, p. 6)—for the sake of obtaining its goods, rapidly rising in price under the combined pressure of increasing demand and diminishing supply. At the very time Europe wanted to buy more goods from South and East Asia, the nomadic conquerors of the overland trade routes levied heavy taxes upon the traffic. Three alternative routes invited investigation—(1) north around Europe, (2) south around Africa, and (3) west around the Earth. All of them were seaways. That to the north was found to be obstructed by ice, although attempts to penetrate it never ceased. That to the south was made difficult by the long, arid and harborless coast of the Sahara and the disease-ridden, rainy, forested coastlands beyond. This southern route nevertheless turned out to be the most direct of the three.

Exploration and Discovery

Explorations both to north and to south could perhaps have been made simply by hugging the coast, but they were greatly facilitated by the recent introduction of the mariner's compass and the sextant. These instruments permitted point-to-point sailing, and even open-sea navigation, as in Da Gama's famous voyage across the Indian Ocean, where he took advantage, both going and returning, of the monsoon (*i. e.* seasonal) winds.

Without the new instruments, exploration westward across the Atlantic could not have been attempted. Of different character but equal importance in the later Middle Ages was a revival among scholars of a belief that the earth was spherical. Owing to the interposition of the long double-continent of the Americas, the westward route did not lead directly to Asia, as had been assumed, but the hypothesis of sphericity proved sound. Clearly both the devising of new instruments and the revival of geographical concepts were prerequisites to the voyages of Columbus. Finally, the shift of interest from otherworldly concerns, the rebirth of classical learning, and the new practice of the scientific observation of nature, all contributed to the Discoveries. Such dynamic combinations of ideas are typical of the Modern Age, and in a real sense distinguish it from the learned but otherworldly Medieval epoch.

The romantic explorations which led to the discovery of Africa, Asia, and the two Americas in less than a century (all, save the west coast of Africa, within a single decade), burst upon the world with such force that they have ever since been called simply "The Discoveries." They were in fact the spectacular announcement that a new age had flowered, an age made possible by the profound but unostentatious changes that had been going on for several centuries.

One Ocean; Several Continents

The overseas expansion that followed upon the Discoveries created a new world, in which Europe remained dominant, but no longer isolated. The gradual assimilation of the civilizations of the several continents to each other has profoundly affected the life of all of them—Europe no less than the others.

The most immediate result of the explorations was the meteoric rise of overseas commerce and the associated stimulus to internal European trade and to urban life. This has been called the Commercial Revolution. Less obvious and more gradual, but no less drastic, came a change from the simple agricultural system of the Middle Ages to a variety of systems, inherently more complex, and varying from region to region in conformity with differences in soil, terrain, and climate—the so-called Agricultural Revolution. Farming in Europe became increasingly affected by crops grown in the world outside Europe—some in competition, others as supplements. At the same time the commercial cities, expanding under the new influences, offered new near-by markets for farm produce, and this in turn led to further specialization in farming. Finally, the alteration in economic and social life implied in the Commercial and Agricultural Revolutions was influenced by the slow political evolution in Europe from a manorial, feudal society into sovereign national states.

All these transformations had begun before the Discoveries expanded the world from a continent to a globe. They were completed at different times in different regions of Europe, and it took centuries for any one of them to make its way from one end of the continent to the other. Operating together they created the

European world which today we call "modern," but which at this very moment gives evidence of transmuting itself into a still different structure.

THE AGRICULTURAL REVOLUTION

No development differentiates the Medieval from the Modern period more decisively than the changed mode of using farmland.

New Farmland

From the eleventh century onwards, population and the standard of living in Europe persistently increased in spite of drastic setbacks due to wars, famines, floods, and pestilences. This expanding population required more and better food and at the same time provided the labor to obtain it.

Bit by bit farmland was reclaimed. Brush and forest were cleared for crops or pasture, until most of the gentler lands were open, leaving only rough terrain and infertile soils under tree growth. An exception to this tendency was the demesne forests of the more powerful landlords, including kings, who kept blocks of woodland for hunting, often arbitrarily selected for personal convenience regardless of the utility of the land for other purposes. Many of these preserves survived into recent times, notably in Britain.

Wet lands were drained wherever possible. In this manner flood-plains along streams, and parts of coastal plains bordering the sea, were converted into rich pastures or exceptionally fertile fields. Irrigation ditches were reopened throughout the Mediterranean world, and in the Iberian Peninsula Christian states fell heir to Moorish irrigation districts, some of which appear to have been more cunningly designed than any the Romans had operated.

As the arable land in Western Europe available for reclamation dwindled, the mounting demand for tillable soil led to expansion into country hitherto occupied only by wandering tribes. By the twelfth century the coniferous forests of the North Central European plain were already being cut, and the marshes left by the continental ice-sheet were being drained.

These activities took place immediately in the rear of the armed Germans who were pushing back, exterminating, or incorporating the aboriginal Slavic inhabitants, as the thrust toward the east (*Drang nach Osten*) swept on. Professional woodsmen found their way to the promising new colonizations from older communities throughout northern Europe, where they and their ancestors had relentlessly felled forests for generations. The more specialized work of draining marshes was done largely by men from the lower Rhine, whose tradition had been to cope with flowlands of floodplain and delta. As new lands were laid under the plow or converted to pasture, the familiar farm system of Western Europe was established, and the frontier progressed eastward precisely as did the west-moving frontier of North America centuries later.

Population Pressure on the Land. While Europe east of the ancient frontier line along the Elbe, the Bohemian mountains, and the Eastern Alps was being conquered and stamped with a modified agricultural pattern derived from the older Europe west of that line, conditions in Western Europe conspired to make farming less and less attractive as a vocation.

In district after district, reclamation of all the readily arable land and its tillage under the three-field system closed local outlets for the increasing population. This heightened two evils already prevalent. (1) Chronic undernourishment became more widespread, and this made the people more than ever susceptible to famine. These occurred whenever floods, drouth, or blight suddenly and drastically reduced the local food supply, because society lacked organized means of producing and storing a surplus, distributing the risk of loss, and repairing the devastation which then as now was universally called an "act of God." (2) Pestilences, like famines, were all too familiar. They ran their course through the population of one district or another at irregular but frequent intervals. Less often they ravaged the whole continent. Nobody understood their source, and few suspected the communicability of diseases or understood the virtues of sanitation.

Fresh Opportunity for Peasants. Driven by adversity to seek other means of subsistence than the traditional medieval agriculture, people found their horizon extended both literally and figuratively. Small surpluses of certain commodities tended to accumulate in districts especially fitted to produce them. Examples were wool in the hilly grazing lands of Italy and England, a frontier country, salt from mines or springs at various spots in Central Europe, fish from the North Sea, and nuts and fruits in the Mediterranean Basin. Some of these commodities, even in their natural state, were ready to join the stream of trade from the untamed northeast and from the exotic Orient. Others could be turned into trade goods by simple processes of manufacture. As traders increased in number, tales they told spread rapidly among farm laborers—now becoming eager to escape heavy and disheartening toil—until even stagnant backwaters were increasingly aware of a great world beyond the hills, the woods, the marshes, or the sea that had heretofore isolated them.

At the close of the eleventh century new outlets for pent-up energy appeared. People hitherto chained to the soil, by ignorance and lack of opportunity even more than by law, learned that Crusades against the infidel were afoot. Some took the Cross, others merely fell in with the rabble that hung on the fringes of these military thrusts to the Levant. Others heard that new farmlands were being seized from heathen nearer home, in central and eastern Europe, whither land-hunger enticed many sober men who were unwilling to join the rash venture of an overseas Crusade.

Still nearer home, towns devoted to trade and handicrafts were growing up, where an industrious man might earn a livelihood, and perhaps amass a competence. Freemen could leave the land without legal hindrance, once they had the vision of a world outside and funds to reach it. Serfs who could avoid detection "for a year and a day" in a free town were by custom loosed from their servile bonds. The growing towns, needing labor, generally welcomed recruits without close investigation. Lay and church lords, eager to absorb raw frontier land, unabashedly advertised for hands, and offered a tacit liberation from outraged masters to any men who were willing to undergo the risks of living on a fluctuating frontier of conquest. Such calls must have been heeded chiefly by the more vigorous and venturesome young pioneers, just as in North America during the eighteenth and nineteenth centuries.

Labor Shortage and Land Enclosure. The effect of all these factors was to produce a net decrease of farm labor in older Europe, to the detriment of the labor-consuming three-field system. At the same time the rising flow of commerce encouraged exchange of products, so that many districts could partially abandon subsistence agriculture for products with sales value. Wool and hides were commodities in demand in the towns where handicrafts were being pushed. Livestock to produce wool and hides required less care than tilled fields. It was only natural, therefore, that landlords encroached upon the common pasture, and even upon plow land, for a new purpose, namely, to provide grazing for cattle, sheep, or goats. Thus they could enlarge their income and solve their labor problem at the same time.

Goats were generally raised in the driest parts of the Mediterranean World, because they can subsist on less and poorer food than other domestic animals. Elsewhere about the Mediterranean sheep were preferred, and they were also common on the heaths, downs, and other hill lands of Britain and France—lands where porosity of the soil or steep slopes kept the ground fairly dry even after abundant rains. On moister lands cattle were the favored livestock.

Everywhere the effect was to take over for the landlord's benefit, land formerly used by free farmers, many of whom therefore found themselves without means of livelihood. Few hands were needed to watch the stock, and often the pastures were fenced. More and more as the Middle Ages wore on, did enclosure of the land destroy the subsistence of an important fraction of the rural population, forcing whole families to find work elsewhere. These landless folk took an important part in the colonization along the eastern frontier, in the rise of towns, and later in overseas settlement.

Improved Use of Rural Land

Enclosure of commons and open fields worked temporary hardship upon great numbers of people, but it laid the foundation for an improved agricultural system. Under the new order, as soon as livestock was kept in large numbers the amount of available manure was sufficient to benefit the soil. It came to be common practice to turn pastures thus fertilized into plowland every few years. During the winter, animals were likely to be confined to barnyards, and the manure accumulated could be spread on the fields just before planting when it would yield maximum benefit.

The soil of most parts of Western Europe responds quickly and well to fertilization, and manuring made it no longer necessary to leave any of the land fallow. This increased the productive acreage by half, and brought to an end the regime of three fields. Much of the acreage gained could be used for hay or other feed crops to tide the livestock over the lean season. Draft beasts could now be kept in good condition throughout the year, and so could work the land more effectively, especially in the critical spring plowing.

A rotation practice was evolved in which pasture for a number of years was followed by wheat or other staple food grain for one or two seasons, then by a planting of varied and less important crops for food and feed, and finally by a few years of hay, before turning in the stock to pasture the deteriorating hayfield. Such a scheme was flexible enough to permit adaptation to suit a wide range of climate, slope, drainage, and soil. Farmers learned that even on the same holding different pieces of land demanded different treatment. The thrifty and intelligent man could now improve his land at will within rather wide limits set by nature. Consequently, management of the arable land as separate, individual plots was substituted for uniform handling of the whole acreage of a manor.

The long-standing subdivision of the holdings into narrow strips adopted to serve the three-field system, proved awkward and inefficient under the new order, in which each farmer decided what crops he could best raise. The narrow untilled strips (balks) between the holdings required by medieval practice, wasted a considerable fraction of arable land, and no one holding was large enough by itself to fence for pasture. In the course of time, exchange, purchase, and reallotment by law eliminated most of the narrow strip-holdings, although they were to be seen in parts of East Central Europe until after World War II.

The Agricultural Revolution began in Western Europe and slowly worked its way eastward. Much of it has taken place since the beginning of the Modern Period. European society first became acutely aware of the need for an improved agricultural system in England and France after the Black Death in the mid-fourteenth century. That plague reduced the population by one-third in a single year, and subsequently still more. So diminished was the laboring class that much land unravaged by war lay idle. Enclosure for sheep pasture thereupon became so common that many farm laborers were in turn forced off the land and had to move to the frontier or to the towns. The ultimate consequence was a new mode of agricultural life for all of Europe, old and new.

[63]

This change in farming accompanied and stimulated improvements in transportation. So long as transport was slow and costly only the least perishable and most valuable products could be sent beyond the market town of the producing district. Lack of a wide market restricted the list of crops a farmer could profitably raise, forced him to produce nearly everything used by his family, and limited his purchasing power proportionally. The shift from medieval to modern farming involved the replacement of subsistence agriculture by commercial production. This could occur only with enhanced opportunity for exchange. The farm system which emerged during the Modern Age took advantage of the wide variety of climate and soil that characterizes Europe, in order to specialize on crops adapted to different regions and to exchange the resulting surpluses. The medieval era of subsistence agriculture had permitted Europe's notable natural diversity to count for little.

THE COMMERCIAL REVOLUTION

In its usually accepted sense the Commercial Revolution occurred after the Discoveries, rather than before them. Obviously, overseas trade could not exist until the great ocean thoroughfare had been discovered. Nevertheless, changes of real import had begun well before the fifteenth century, affecting the radius, the variety, and the volume of trade. As farm surpluses began to increase with the tendency to specialize in the production of crops according to the regions best suited for them, the volume of agricultural commodities in commerce increased, and even today remains large. But Europe pulled itself up very slowly from its old local self-sufficiency to a modern exchange economy. During the early Middle Ages the Roman roads had largely ceased to function as parts of a Europe-wide transport system. Their pavements disappeared, many segments became grass-grown or incorporated into private properties. Such long-haul business as there was had to take to routes provided by nature—primarily rivers and coastal waters. The headwaters of navigable streams were linked by arduous portage routes, some of them over mountain passes. As always in a period of backward technology, medieval man remained closely dependent upon his natural environment.

During the century or two before the Discoveries, main transport routes conformed to the major riverways and to coasting routes in the protected inland seas (Fig. 6, p. 36). Local traffic, moving only a few miles, doubtless made up a large fraction of the goods and persons carried. Trunkline business, confined to the less bulky and more valuable luxury goods and to the occasional movement of persons, was geographically more significant, because it determined the primary pattern of main routes along which favorably located towns grew into cities.

Trade with the North

Two exotic areas acted like magnetic fields to attract traders and create trade routes across the heart of Europe. To the north lay the frontier. Its products were not notably valuable, but they could be had for little in exchange, as is always true of frontier regions. Wool from pastoral Britain, and beeswax, hair, pelts, and amber from the forested continent were characteristic frontier products. With Britain and Scandinavia intercourse was maintained by small boats plying across narrow straits and bays small and large (Fig. 8, p. 66). Ports on both sides of these dividing waters could be established in the many deep harbors provided by a coastline where the river mouths have been drowned, their valleys filled by broad inlets penetrating inland dozens of miles and kept free from silt by tidal scour. Nearly every ancient port of North Europe stands at the head of tidewater, where a trading town could profit from three advantages: maximum penetration inland by cheaply operated sailing ships; location far enough inland to be reasonably safe from the pirates of the high seas; the overland crossing farthest downstream (in effect, the coast road). Such of the rivers as were navigable provided a fourth advantage: easy connection with the interior by river craft. Rouen, Ghent, Cologne, Bremen, Hamburg, Lübeck, Stettin, Danzig, Stockholm, Oslo, and London have characteristic locations at estuary heads (Fig. 8, p. 66).

The frontier was linked to the Mediterranean by the long and easily navigated north-flowing rivers—Seine, Rhine, Weser, Elbe, Oder, and Vistula—and their connections across the Alps or down the Rhône Valley. The Rhône is a swift and treacherous stream, but was much used for downstream traffic; goods moving north were likely to be carried overland on highways following the valley, at least during highest and lowest water. Elsewhere traffic in the Mediterranean coastlands moved overland at all seasons be-

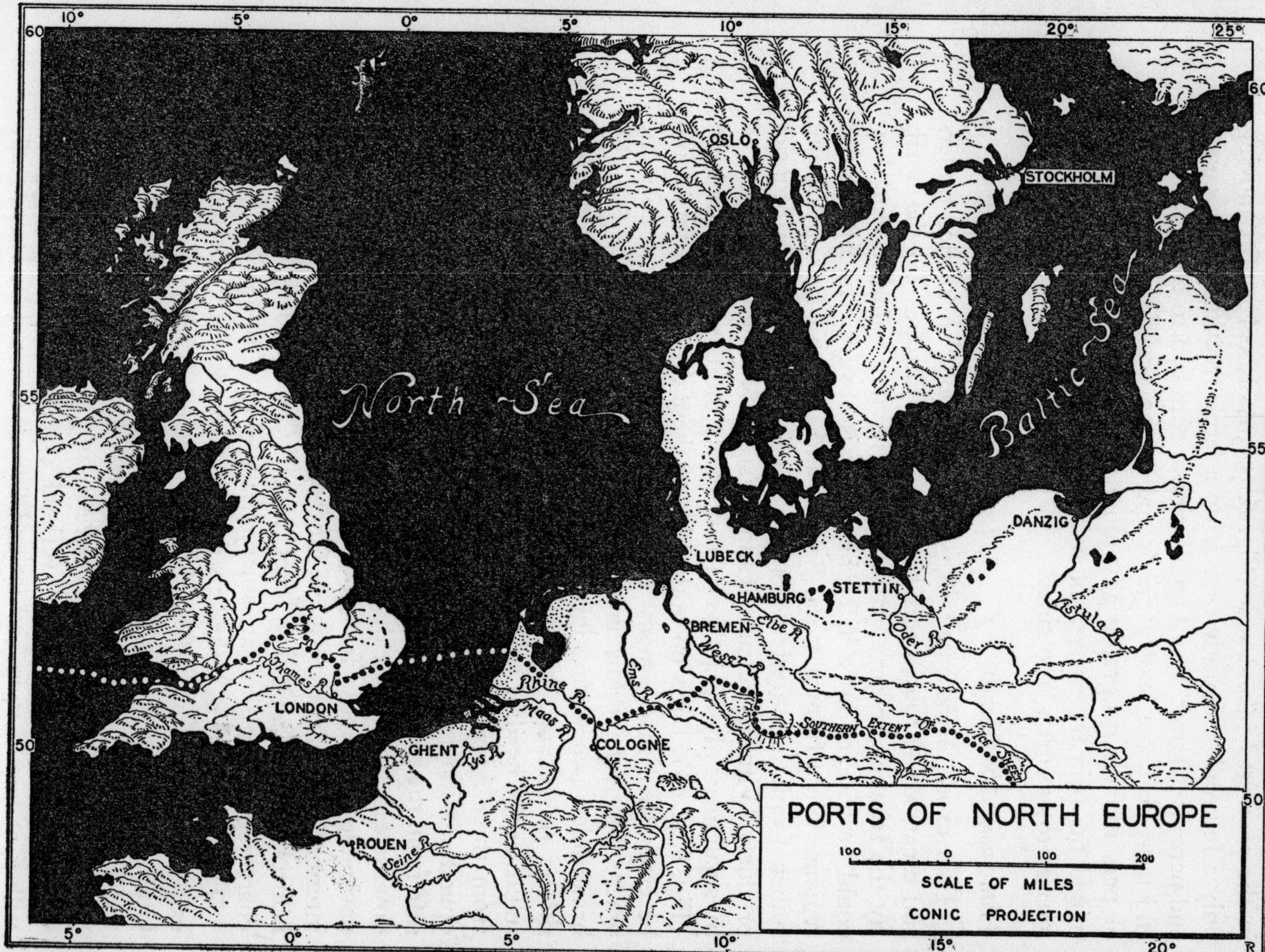

FIG. 8. LEADING EARLY PORTS OF NORTH EUROPE.

PORTS OF NORTH EUROPE

SCALE OF MILES

CONIC PROJECTION

cause the streams were small and short, and they fluctuated from dangerous winter floods to treacherous summer shallows.

Trade with the East

The second "magnetic field" of medieval European commerce was the Levant (the eastern end of the Mediterranean Sea), to which goods from still farther east found their way by overland routes (Figs. 2, p. 6, and 3, p. 10). Until the Turks took possession of the Byzantine Empire a short time before the Discoveries, Constantinople was the major western terminus of the Oriental trade, with Antioch and Tripoli (Syria) as lesser ports. These places lie at or connect with the end of the age-old trade route that runs in a great crescent between the Arabian Desert and the mountains at the base of the Asia Minor Peninsula. Of the ports serving this trade, only Constantinople was favored with a commodious and protected harbor.

The direct route from Constantinople to Central and Western Europe involved either much overland travel through rugged country or use of the Danube River. This swift stream was navigable but it traversed open plains, the scene of intermittent fighting between the Austro-Hungarians and nomads from Eurasia. The Mediterranean sea route was preferred on every count, and the traffic fell more and more largely into the hands of Italian port cities. Venice and Genoa, at the Mediterranean outlets of principal Alpine pass routes, came to be the dominant trading states. Each had a harbor satisfactory for ships of the period, and each grew into a wealthy and powerful country by serving as middleman to the trade.

Not all the business of the Byzantine and Italian cities was in goods. At intervals they profited greatly by transporting Crusaders to Palestine, and in the periods between Crusades Italians did a humbler but larger business in taking pilgrims to Rome from all parts of the Mediterranean region.

European Internal Trade

Far greater in volume than either the oriental or the frontier trade, was the traffic between Mediterranean Europe and North Europe. Both were long-settled regions, they had been parts of a single civilization for many centuries, and during most of this period the Roman Church and the Latin tongue had given the whole area, save for the Balkan Peninsula, enough unity to facilitate interchange of goods, persons, and ideas. Nevertheless, the Mediterranean section never lost the traditions of the classical period as completely as did North Europe, and nearly all the daring new movements that ushered in Modern History—ocean commerce, manufacturing, the Renaissance, and the Discoveries—first took shape in Mediterranean lands, and afterward spread northward. These contrasting developments created an economic foundation for vigorous trade between the areas. Above all, these two parts of Europe are distinguished from each other by climates so different that their commerce in agricultural products has proved permanently reciprocal.

Trading Towns. The port towns on the Italian coast and in North Europe shared in the trade based on the differences between South and North Europe, but as terminals rather than as way stations. Between them lay inland towns devoted to this overland trade and to handicrafts that contributed to it.

Earliest in the field were towns of north Italy—the Po Plain and the Tuscan and Umbrian hill-lands (Fig. 6, p. 36). Firmly rooted in an ancient tradition of handicraft, and stimulated to new efforts by the display of oriental wares in their markets, these towns came to make textiles, glass, pottery, leatherwork, jewelry, and metal wares of high technical quality and rare artistic merit. These goods were readily sold to the wealthy people in the more backward North Europe. More than a score of Italian towns throve mightily as the Middle Ages began to give place to modern life. The most successful were those which lay at major route foci, and so were able to dominate interregional trade as well as a productive homeland.

A prime example was Florence, which lay where the major passes through the Northern Apennines converged upon a direct road to Rome, and where, besides, this north-south highway crossed the east-west Arno Valley route. Verona was an example of a trading town at the outlet to a major Alpine pass. Milan gathered to itself the trade of half a dozen pass routes where they converge like sticks of a fan from the semicircle of the central and western Alps. Each lesser city possessed some unique advantage: Piacenza controlled the most feasible crossing of the Po between Milan and peninsular Italy; Parma, Bologna, Lucca, and others lay at outlets of notches in the Apennines; Pisa and Leghorn have been the successive seaports of Tuscany.

Profiting similarly from trade and especially from crafts, but later than the Italian centers, many towns of the plains of North Europe in time gained large shares of the growing wealth of the continent. The towns of Champagne were famous trading places, especially Troyes, where the navigable Seine River on its way to Paris crosses the main highway between the Rhône Valley and the English Channel. The rulers of this district had infertile land and made the most of their position on major trade routes by fostering fairs which traders from all Europe eagerly attended. Among the earliest navigation canals in the Occident were those of Champagne, built to facilitate inland transportation. The policy of according legal protection to traders was as enlightened as that which provided physical facilities for them.

The Rhine was perhaps the most important trade route in northern Europe. Its banks were dotted with famous trading points. A few overshadowed the rest: Basel stood at the Great Elbow of the river, Mainz (along with Frankfurt on the tributary Main) on the principal cross-route in its middle course, and Cologne at the head of ocean navigation and on the east-west overland route of the North European Plain. Both the Rhine and the Champagne routes led to the Flemish lowlands, where textile manufacture first took firm root in North Europe. In a remarkably short time the numerous towns of Flanders and adjacent districts were supplying all the country north of the Alps with most of its woolen and linen cloth.

East of the Rhine River the Weser, Elbe, Oder, and Vistula were used for trade. Connections were made southward by roads and trails either toward the passes of the central and eastern Alps, or toward the Middle Danube Plain by way of the Moravian Gate. Magdeburg and Frankfurt-an-der-Oder lay at crossings of riverways and the east-west route of the lowland plain; Nuremberg, Augsburg, Regensburg, Breslau, and Cracow grew up at similar junctions of riverways and highways farther south.

Some seventy-five of the trading towns of the North European Plain between the Rhine and the Vistula gradually formed a loose commercial alliance, the Hanseatic League. They had connections and warehouses in the principal Scandinavian and English ports, on the mainland coast of the Baltic, and at Novgorod, the commercial outpost of Europe in Russia. This gave the League control of most of the frontier trade, and is an example of the integrating force of commerce despite political subdivision.

Where routes crossed the rugged zone that separates South and North Europe, other towns prospered from the trade that passed. Most of them were small, because their agricultural base was small and their commercial functions were restricted. Chur and Chiavenna, within the mountains but at opposite ends of Alpine passes, were examples. On the Rhône similar functions were discharged by two cities of the plain, located at points where the north-south route branched: at Lyons spur routes climbed westward toward the Loire Basin and eastward to Lake Geneva and the upper Rhine Basin; at Dijon the route bifurcated toward Champagne and toward the Middle Rhine. Lyons and Dijon, benefitting also from far richer surroundings than the Alpine towns, took their place on a par with other lowland commercial metropolises.

Minerals and Trade. Contributing to the total commercial turnover was a small but growing trade in minerals. Exchange economy demanded convenient media, and for this purpose gold, and particularly silver, were sought throughout the continent, as was copper for small coins. Lead was in demand for roofs of public buildings, for pewter (the ordinary material for table utensils) and, with the coming of gunpowder, for bullets. Copper and tin kitchen vessels and copper and zinc for brass made demands on the scattered supplies. Iron and steel were used for weapons, including armor, for tools, and for many other common purposes, although the quantity required was much less per capita than at the present time.

Tin could be had only in southwestern England (Fig. 7, p. 50). Small deposits of silver, copper, lead, or zinc were discovered in many places, chiefly in the ancient hill lands and low mountain *massifs*, and often in association. Spain had never ceased to produce these metals. In Central Europe the Harz Mountain district of Germany was the earliest famous producer, reaching its peak about 1000 A.D. Subsequently, miners from the Harz went to the Erzgebirge (Ore Mountains) on the Bohemian frontier, and later generations trekked on to Transylvania, in the eastern Carpathians. Iron was the most widely disseminated metal. Bogs in the humid north contained small accumulations. Underground but shallow mines were opened here and there from Spain and Britain to Italy and Poland. The abundant forests of North Europe furnished local charcoal for smelting, and in South Europe, where wood was scarce, charcoal could be procured from brush-covered mountains not too remote to be drawn upon.

The total volume of minerals that entered trade must have been small. Nevertheless, the strict localization of these commodities affected the layout of routes while their vital importance made their transportation a matter of special concern to merchants and rulers alike. The critical need for minerals in wartime has not changed from the Middle Ages to the present, although the specific metals in demand vary from age to age, with the progress of technology.

Legal Status of Commercial Towns

Not all Europeans who lived by trade fostered it. Many lords, bred in the agricultural tradition, saw in rising trade either a threat to their economic and social world, or else a goose laying golden eggs. Such of these men as controlled strategic bits of trade routes in a position to tap the traffic by taxing it. Ownership of a castle that had been erected for defense on a cliff overlooking a navigable stream, at a narrow mountain pass, or on a natural crossroads, made it possible to levy on all goods and persons using the route. Toll gates on roads and trails, chains across rivers, and tolls at bridges and ferries, were devices used to take a profit from the traffic. Wise rulers kept the taxes low enough to insure continuance of the flow of business. Others laid such heavy taxes that alternative routes were sought and used. If new routes could not be found, the traffic languished under the weight of the payments demanded. In general the larger landholders were least inclined to overtax trade. They had other sources of income, and they were in a position to see the damage excessive taxes might cause. The enlightenment of the Counts of Champagne has already been mentioned. A minor lord, whose fields and pastures could not keep him in comfort, was more likely to snatch greedily at the wealth passing his door. In districts where holdings were generally small, the aggregate levies tended to strangle trade even when individual takings were not excessive. Central Europe presented the paradox of having the most numerous and arbitrary imposts, while at the same time having the most powerful and independent trading towns. As soon as coastwise routes were established, the seaboard towns of this region abandoned the tax-fettered overland routes.

The manorial aristocracy looked down upon commerce, apart from taxing it, as an upstart means of livelihood. Most of the townsmen who engaged in trade were therefore people lacking gentle blood, and as in all new commercial societies, success was as likely to crown ruthlessness and deception as to reward industry and shrewdness. Landlords often felt themselves to be victims of the merchants and moneylenders with whom they did business. Consequently trading towns usually had an uphill fight to obtain from hereditary rulers the grants of privilege necessary for their legal protection.

Where the rulers were relatively strong, as in the extreme west of Europe, cities were given privileges slowly, reluctantly, and often under strict supervision of the king. In Central Europe the burden of the Holy Roman Empire drained the surplus wealth of the successive wearers of the imperial crown. To get funds for the pursuit of the title of Emperor and for subsequent imperial expeditions to Italy, many a successful contestant was impoverished and forced to call upon his urban subjects for loans of money. Such money was rarely repaid, and so was usually forthcoming only in return for a grant of privilege. By obtaining successive privileges many towns in Germany and in Italy came to be independent in all but name.

INCIPIENT "NATIONAL STATES"

The interweaving of the economic, social, and political life of a people never ceases, but the earth-pattern produced varies from age to age and from region to region. The centuries that saw the beginnings of profound alterations in agricultural and commercial pursuits, witnessed also a territorial rearrangement of political units no less far-reaching.

Attempts at Territorial Unity

The Middle Ages inherited from Rome the ideal concept of a World State. The ancient Roman Empire had embraced roughly the civilized Western and Near Eastern (Levantine) world of its

[72]

day. At Constantinople in the Greek-speaking Eastern Roman Empire, the imperial succession continued unbroken until 1453, when that capital fell to the advancing Turks (Fig. 4, p. 12).

A World State. In the Latin West the ideal of political unity survived the Teutonic invasions and the temporary abeyance of the imperial title for some three centuries (476-800). This ideal unity found a dual expression in the West. (1) In the spiritual realm it was expressed in the imperial pretensions and the expanding moral sway of the See of Peter embodied in the person of the Pope, whose prestige derived from his status as Bishop of Rome, the ancient capital of the west. (2) In the secular sphere the imperial tradition was revived in the person of the ruler of the Frankish people.

The Franks, a Germanic folk whose original homeland lay in the Rhine Valley between the delta and the confluence of the Main, founded their imperial claims on the conquest of most of the Rhine and Seine basins. This conquest of the Seine region from a Rhenish base reversed the Roman progress from northern Gaul to the Rhine frontier, but it followed the same natural routes, and anticipated the course of invasion from that day to this (including 1940).

Further expansion and conquest, based on the Rhineland and the Paris Basin, gave the Franks under Charlemagne a brief continental mastery beginning in 800 A.D., that included virtually all of western Christian (*i.e.*, Latin) civilization, except Britain, south Italy, and the bulk of the Iberian Peninsula. The empire barely survived its creator, but the restoration had endowed the imperial title with a prestige that preserved the name, Holy Roman Empire, and lent it a potent influence on the political thought of western mankind for a thousand years.

Shortly after Charlemagne's death, the indisputably Latin lands to the west of the Rhine, and the equally Germanic lands to the east of that valley, began to go their own separate ways. This dual development left a central corridor with fluctuating frontiers, nominally under the imperial sway, but in fact the continuous battleground of the future France and Germany. Here germinated the titanic struggle that still goes on.

This narrow strip of disputed territory may be regarded as extending in practice from the mouth of the Rhine to Rome. The corridor was cut in two by the barrier of the Alps, a serious obstacle to free movement even in summer, and a little-traversed waste in winter. Lacking barriers on any of its frontiers, it never attained fixed territorial or cultural unity. Its chief value lay in the fact that it was a main artery of trade between the south and the north. The early emperors made a vigorous but unsuccessful effort to control this lucrative traffic.

The real power of the emperors was derived from their personal holdings, which lay chiefly in the German part of Europe. Two centuries before the Discoveries the imperial title migrated southward and eastward to the farthest border of the German world. Thereafter it was associated with the House of Hapsburg, whose chief possession was Austria, the Danubian outpost march against the Asiatic tribesmen. Austrian holdings included fertile farmlands and rich mines unified by a network of trade routes centered on Vienna. Besides the east-west route along the Danube itself, this web enmeshed valuable central and eastern Alpine passes, and the Moravian Gate between the Middle Danube Basin and the North European Plain (Fig. 6, p. 36). Elsewhere in the world traditionally associated with the later centuries of the Western Roman Empire, both north and south of the Alps, the ideal of a unified world state was lost in a mosaic of small territories.

Lesser Unities. Meanwhile political ambitions less grandiose than world domination were being achieved. In an age that counted wealth almost exclusively in land, landowners strove mightily to obtain as much territory as possible. In general the ruler who possessed the most farmland could marshall the largest fighting force, and so make himself leader of his district. But landowners great and small were confronted with the stubborn fact that optimum use of land under European conditions of soil and climate, required that it be managed in rather small tracts. It was this fact that brought the small districts, known as manors, into existence as the basic units of agrarian economic life, even before the end of the Roman Empire of the West.

The lord of numerous manors, especially if they were scattered, usually found it necessary to turn some of them over to vassals who could personally supervise their share of the holdings. For use of the land they rendered specified returns, especially military service, to their liege lord. While clinging tenaciously to the traditional ideal of an emperor paramount throughout the civilized world, the various regions of Western Europe took a more realistic attitude toward the immediate problems of local government.

The need was simple—the creation of political units large enough and provided with sufficient natural resources to defend themselves. The process was overlaid with complicated legal conditions, but territorially it entailed the assembling of manors and their market towns into units rich and varied enough to be self-sustaining and self-governing. As centuries passed, a few of these political units outstripped the rest by the simple but effective method of incorporating their neighbors. The procedure has never become obsolete, as is evident in the moves of Germany and Russia into neighboring states during and following World War II. The elements of success in the long sweep of territorial consolidation were social and economic, and sometimes personal, as well as environmental and political.

Assimilation was swifter and less difficult during the earlier era of slight cultural differentiation and fluctuating political boundaries, than later, when linguistic groups had crystallized in semi-isolation, and had acquired material and cultural resources with which to resist incorporation into a more powerful state. Three examples will illustrate this point.

Fusion of the district around Orléans with the Île-de-France in the early years of the French monarchy, amounted to little more than an extension of a uniform administration over adjacent tracts of about equal size and value, occupied by peoples who dwelt in much the same sort of country and spoke virtually the same dialect. Some centuries later a French state that had demonstrated its vigor by forcibly eliminating English and Burgundian authority from large tracts of French-speaking territory, and had already amalgamated most of the area known today as France, conquered Brittany. This was a small outlying district handicapped by rugged and rocky terrain, infertile soil, and a wet, cool climate; but it derived coherence from the distinctiveness and unity of its peninsula, and the reliance of most of its inhabitants upon fishing combined with supplemental farming. Today, after nearly 500 years as part of France, the Bretons conserve their language and their costume, and are not whole-heartedly French.

Until the Netherlands was overrun in 1940 by military force, the Dutch kept themselves independent of Germany. For two centuries they had lived under the shadow of a far larger Teutonic state, and for twice that period they had been middlemen in the overseas trade of the whole German area. But long before that, they had evolved a distinct language in the isolation of their marshy delta, they had continued to live a highly individualized life in ceaseless struggle with the waters of their amphibious habitat, and an important part of their national energy was devoted to overseas commerce and colonial developments—activities carried on in an environment which Germany could not reach, so long as it remained a disunited group of inland states. With Germany defeated in 1945, the Netherlands reverted to its traditional independence of its large neighbor.

Many small states persisted, especially in the part of Central Europe where the Roman imperial legend survived longest, because central authority had been too weak to consolidate them. When powerful and jealous neighbors grew up on the west and on the east, they made it their policy to prevent union within the intermediate zone. This was very apparent in northern and central Italy. There for ages the Emperors and the Popes had struggled for supremacy. After the imperial pretension was finally extinguished in battles of 1250 A.D. on the hot and malarial Po Plain, France and Austria waged war after war for dominance in Italy. In the twentieth century this struggle was transformed into rivalry between France and Germany for Italian support, which made its latest appearance in World War II.

Emerging National Diversity

Nearly everyone of the larger and more powerful states of the epoch when the Middle Ages were fading into the modern period, identified itself with a single language and nationality. These national states typified the modern age. Most of them added territory by fighting or by being ready to fight. Even when land fell to them through marriage, inheritance, or purchase, they had to be prepared to fight for its retention. The most successful states may have fought more vigorously than the rest, but they profited from possessing some inherent long-term advantage. Such an advantage might be occupancy of a naturally defended terrain which was fertile, and perhaps also lay on profitable trade routes or near enough to tap them. The possession of mineral wealth was a minor supplementary asset in a few cases (Fig. 7, p. 50).

In Northwest Europe. France grew from the Île-de-France as a nucleus and had Paris as a focus. The immediately surrounding country was fertile, and the Seine and other navigable river systems brought moderate trade to the capital city. The outstanding military advantage of this small, original holding of the Capetian rulers was its position at the center of half a dozen concentric lines of hills, each rising gradually outward toward the northeast, east, and south, and presenting a steep and rugged face to the invaders. This multiple military barrier of encircling hills enabled the rulers of France to ward off enemies century after century, while steadily pushing their borders outward. In the course of this expansion they annexed the profitable Champagne trade route, as well as much farmland (Figs. 9, p. 78, and 6, p. 36).

England likewise expanded from an urban center partly shielded by similar concentric lines of hills. These were minor items in its defense and territorial expansion compared to the tremendous advantage derived from insularity. The North Sea and the English Channel kept the country inviolate from invasion so long as British seapower went unchallenged. At the same time, these "narrow seas" and the wider oceans gave to England opportunities for colonization and trade which, in the course of time, produced the British Empire. Scandinavia and the Low Countries are seats of smaller states that fell into the general pattern of England, with local variations due chiefly to incomplete physical separation from the continent.

Other vigorous states of the early modern epoch gained their dominant position by fighting to bolster natural defenses of a secondary order. They include the nations of Iberia and eastern Germany (Fig. 9, p. 78).

In Southwest Europe. Portugal and the small units that finally coalesced to form Spain, emerged from fortress-like habitats in the Cantabrian and Pyrenees mountains, to grow into relentless and warlike states on the bleak plateaus and barren hills of the northern half of Iberia. Fired by Christian zeal to oust the Moslem conquerors from their homeland, these small states pushed slowly southward in an intermittent crusade lasting seven centuries, until the peninsula was finally cleared in the very year that Columbus

FIG. 9. CORES, DIRECTIONS OF EXPANSION, AND FIFTEENTH

CENTURY LIMITS OF EUROPEAN NATIONAL STATES

discovered America. In the process all of their people intermingled on the open plateau of the interior, except the Portuguese of the Atlantic lowland and the Catalans of the Ebro Basin. A major distinction between these two flanking regions and the bulk of the Iberian Peninsula is their lowland character and the ease with which they make contact with the sea for fishing and for trading. In contrast, the other coastal lowlands of the peninsula are narrow fringes at the base of the interior "Meseta." This is a high, dry, barren, and mountain-crossed plateau, the chief natural resource of which is its minerals.

Such a contrast between lowland and upland environments could be a source of strength to a unified state if autonomy were conceded to its reciprocal environmental components. Nowhere else in Europe is the delicate balance between separatism and union so neatly illustrated. The Meseta countries, as they expanded southward on the upland, coalesced into a political unity that has never been shattered in spite of regional variations that persist. This is partly true even where the population is totally different in both origin and language, as in the mountainous Basque country. Catalonia, differing in dialect and lying mainly in a broad lowland, early attached itself to the dominant group, partly because it lay in the path of territorial expansion. After five centuries, however, both these districts retain their language and their national feeling. In 1936 they formed the backbone of the losing side in a civil war which from the viewpoint of political geography was a struggle between centralized authority and demands for local autonomy. Portugal, lying outside the main line of expansion, carried on its own thrust against the Moors on the broad Atlantic coastal plain. Its efforts were crowned with success more than two hundred years before the larger task of Spain was accomplished. When Spain finally annexed the smaller country by force, in the century following the Discoveries, its distinctive language was already set, its traditions at home and abroad constituted a rallying point for the assertion of Portuguese nationality, and the union was dismembered after only sixty years.

In Eastern North Europe. In east central Europe coherent states of moderate size grew up along the line of contact between Germanic and Slavic societies. Two of these states were of German origin, and stood on the open routes between the stable west and the fluid east. Both were established during the Middle Ages as outposts of a sedentary society against the threat of raids by roving migrants from the east. Austria occupied the gap made by the Danube between the Alps and the lesser, but effective barrier of wooded ranges known as the Bohemian Forest and the Erzgebirge. Saxony and Prussia are the modern heirs of several border "march" states on the North European Plain between these ranges and the Baltic Sea. In this discussion Saxony may be disregarded, because Prussia became dominant in the whole plains area. Both Austria and Prussia were condemned by location to a constant state of readiness to fight in defense of Germany. It was natural that such states should use their military machine to carry on aggression against their enemies.

Step by step the German border was pushed eastward. Austria imposed Germanic culture upon its neighbors without suppressing their individuality. This was natural because they occupied definite and defensible territories, which could be penetrated by cultural influences more readily than conquered by military force. The Bohemian and Moravian Slavs, lodged behind the Bohemian Forest and the Erzgebirge, were semi-Germanized before the end of the Middle Ages. The Hungarians of the grassy plain of the Middle Danube maintained a nomadic tradition of horsemanship and stock-raising, but they had also become sedentary enough to build a Gothic cathedral in their capital city in the fourteenth century.

In contrast to Austria, Prussia pursued a policy of ingesting small territorial units. In each such district the Slavic natives were either killed or completely Germanized. No vestige of Slavic culture remains on the north European Plain east of Poland except in two districts. In the sandlands and marshes of the upper Spree Valley (a very inaccessible and poverty-stricken region during the period of conquest), a few Wends still spoke their Slavic tongue until World War II, a cultural island in a Prussian sea. In the rugged and infertile hills of Pomerelia a similar small group spoke a dialect closely resembling Polish. But this district lay close to the Polish frontier and at times has been incorporated in a Polish state.

A little prior to the Discoveries, the Germanic expansion eastward came to a halt. In the Middle Danube Basin the Hungarians, though Christianized, maintained quasi-independence until their sovereignty was snuffed out, not by Austrians pushing downstream, but by Turks surging upstream. On the North European Plain the Polish state, at the time entrenched against Prussian aggression behind a double barrier of marshes, established its independence, but accepted Roman Catholicism and many other features of Western European culture. Farther east, beyond peninsular Europe, Russia was throwing off the yoke of Asiatic nomads, and laying the foundations of a settled national state. Meanwhile overseas exploration was progressing under the aegis of Iberian and Scandinavian states.

EUROPE'S TERRITORIAL PATTERN

Thus, in the early fifteenth century the broad territorial pattern of Europe already resembled the political map of the 1930's. Most of the national states of modern Europe had taken form around their nuclei, leaving only their borderlands to be shaped by later drawing of boundary lines. The notable exception was Central Europe, where from the North Sea to Sicily, the territory lay broken into political units of every size from the single community to the huge, inchoate, sprawling assembly headed by Austria. Few of these political units had barrier boundaries, and none of the larger ones consisted of a single, uninterrupted block of territory. In this middle zone the map continued to look like that of the Middle Ages.

To the east and to the west, states were generally of moderate or even large size, several of them possessed barrier boundaries, at least in part, and all but two or three comprised single blocks of territory. There remained small enclaves of foreign sovereignty here and there, but they constituted no threat to the territorial integrity of the states in which they were embedded. Most of these states were internally coherent as social groups, as well. Each had sprung from an organizing nucleus around which territorial accretion had begun, and continued. In such states the peripheral inhabitants usually recognized the dialect of its nucleus as the national vernacular, because it was spoken by the ruler. However, until the invention of printing (in the mid-fifteenth century) variations in spelling and pronunciation were of little consequence among people who read little and travelled hardly at all.

In the course of the Middle Ages, under the spell of a common heritage and the stimulus of a common struggle against foreign enemies, the intangible but powerful force of nationalism had been born in most, if not all, of the larger states of westernmost Europe. So far, nationality has turned out to be the most powerful integrating force in modern political society. Indeed, it might not be far wrong to consider the birth of nationality in any given state as the moment of its transmutation from a medieval to a modern institution.

Territorial Advantages of the National State

The national state had certain territorial advantages over its medieval predecessor. It was obviously larger than any of its constituent units. Even in the poorest regions increase in area meant some increase in resources. This was sure to be an advantage, but it might be especially valuable through incorporation of resources reciprocal with those in the nuclear core of the state. For example, the original territory of France was an agricultural land in which trade was a minor and incidental business. The addition of Champagne, an infertile farmland, brought France astride a major European trade route. Later the accretion of a length of Mediterranean seacoast gave the growing nation a contrasting climate and increased its commercial potential, especially in agricultural products.

Another advantage of territorial enlargement and rearrangement was the reduction of the length of boundaries. Typical medieval states comprised scattered units which were costly to defend at best, and at worst were virtually held in pawn by the rulers of intervening territory. The assemblage of scattered units into a single uninterrupted block reduced the task of boundary defense and gave the strength of unity to the whole aggregation of the nation's natural resources.

The energy released by this process was incalculable. Most national states had no sooner perfected their internal structure than they launched a program of expansion. The direction in which this energy moved was determined by opportunity. The states of East Central Europe began waging wars upon each other in order to obtain maximum territory on the extensive and indeterminate plains of that part of the continent. Austria was soon embroiled in struggles with the advancing Turks on the east, and with West European states along the Franco-German border, where imperial claims

[83]

demanded or permitted intervention. The national states fronting the Atlantic Ocean generally devoted their surplus energy to overseas exploration, and later to colonization of the lands which were discovered. Intermittently they plunged into war with one another over these colonial spoils.

Europe of the Fifteenth Century

The map of Europe in the epoch of the Discoveries reveals a continent in which most of the states of subsequent centuries were adumbrated, but where considerable areas still bore close resemblance to the minuter subdivision of the preceding era. It was a continent which included the Baltic countries and Poland as the utmost extension of its culture, including religion, to the eastward. Its southern margin was not yet fully cleared of Moslem invaders in the southwest, and their coreligionists had not begun to be driven back in the southeast. The African and Asiatic shores of the Mediterranean Sea were wholly independent of European control and cut off from European culture.

Already intellectual, economic, and political ferments of profound significance had begun to alter the ways in which people occupied land, and these changes went hand-in-hand with territorial rearrangements in the political world. Some of the changes were made possible or accelerated by the revival of classical learning, and by inventions which lifted material technology to a new level.

Improved methods of farming utilized the land more efficiently, partly by taking account of regional differences in climate and of local variation in soil and in exposure to sun and wind. Surpluses, accumulated through wiser land-use, stimulated exchange between areas reciprocal in products. Each region increased its output by specializing. Trading towns grew up at junctions and crossings of routes, and at points where goods and people had to shift from one form of transport to another. The people who lived in the towns and engaged in trade provided an additional market for farm produce. Handicrafts sprang up under the magic of improved transportation for raw materials and finished goods, and the artisans swelled urban populations.

The axis of trade and of mercantile towns reached from the Mediterranean between Venice and Marseilles to the North Sea

(Fig. 6, p. 36). To the eastward lay the expanding frontier, and along it were the nuclei of several states destined to become larger than most of those to the westward, in keeping with the larger scale of the landscape. Apart from larger size, the character of most of those states was medieval, rather than modern. Few of them had been stirred by the ferments that were at work in Western Europe. In contrast, states of the Atlantic border had achieved a marked degree of territorial unity and coherence, even where their outlines were not yet filled out. They stood at different stages on the way to modern utilization of the land, but all had set out upon the road. The energy they conserved by modernization found no outlet on an expanding frontier, except in southern Spain, and there the work was all but finished. Instead it was available for exploration and colonization overseas, and toward those objectives much of it was directed.

All of the colonizing states on the Atlantic periphery of Europe had considerable populations devoted to fishing (Fig. 10, p. 86). The waters on the shallow banks off Western Europe were cool and therefore teemed with firm-fleshed fish suitable for curing to supply a substitute for meat on fast days, and a cheap protein food during the season when farm products were scarce. Crews for merchant ships could be recruited from fishing fleets, and as navies grew up, the fishermen made hardy and experienced sailors for warships. Fishing vessels on the banks of Iceland, Newfoundland, and Morocco pointed the way to the routes later followed in the Discoveries.

The Atlantic coast of Europe was well supplied with harbors of every size and suited to every use. Fishing fleets preferred to be based close to the fishing grounds, even where only small coves were available. Merchant ships sailed into harbors as far inland as possible, in order to load and unload near the populous core of the country. Naval vessels could be segregated in commodious but secluded harbors more serviceable to them than to commercial ventures.

Environmental Inequality

The several European coastal states from Norway to Portugal varied in size and wealth. They were even more unequally matched for the race to colonial power in less obvious ways. Probably no

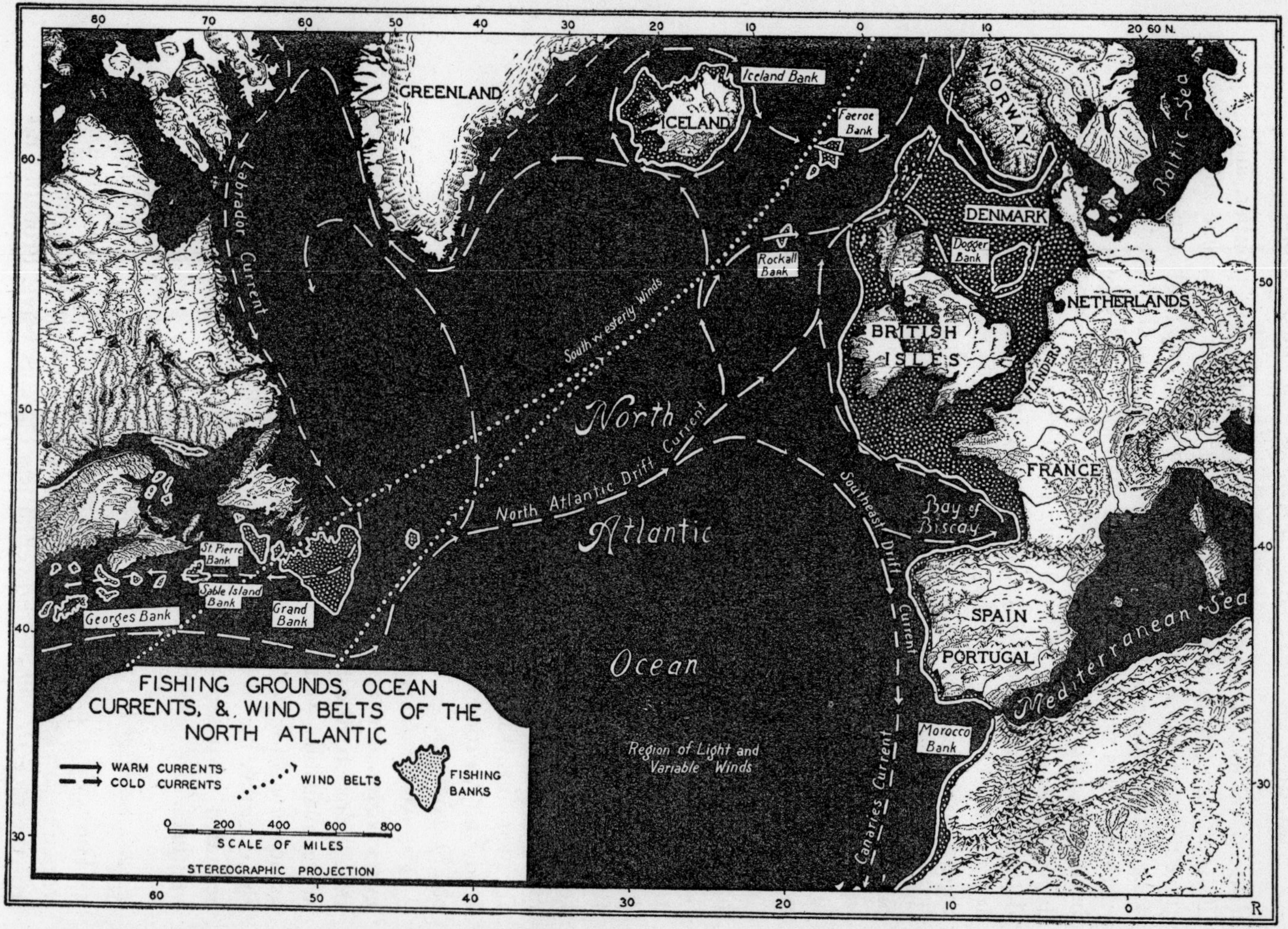

FIG. 10. FISHING GROUNDS, OCEAN CURRENTS, AND WIND BELTS OF THE NORTH ATLANTIC.

one living in 1450 could have correctly forecast the actual course of modern imperial development.

Norway and Denmark had been recently joined in political union, but their equipment for overseas exploration and colonization differed. Norway was the most exclusively maritime region in Europe. Its climate was cold, its relief mountainous, its soil infertile, and much of the interior had been scraped by glaciers to bare bedrock. Its hundreds of little harbors and the abundant fish off-shore turned every generation of Norwegians to the sea for a livelihood. They early undertook exploration along the north coast of the continent, but were balked by the drifting ice which perpetually blockaded the shore east of the White Sea (Fig. 2, p. 6). They moved across the foggy north Atlantic by way of stepping-stone islands—Faeroes, Iceland, and Greenland (Fig. 10). If they reached the North American mainland centuries before the era of the recognized discoveries, they left no indisputable record of their finds.

In contrast to Norway, Denmark had no satisfactory harbors on its west (Atlantic) side. It was a moderately productive lowland facing east at the gateway to the Baltic Sea, and profited from the trade which passed its door. It had no urgent incentive to become an important maritime state beyond this limited radius, although it did venture into the competition for overseas trade.

The two states of the Iberian Peninsula were likewise similar in location and very different in other respects. They lay closer than the rest of Europe to the African coastal route which proved to be the shortest natural route to the Orient, but this advantage was reduced by the fact that they were cut off from the rest of Europe by distance and by the Pyrenees Mountains.

Portugal was a small country of infertile soil. As in Norway, many of its people turned to the sea for a livelihood, attracted by the presence of richer resources there than on land. Its interests therefore have always been maritime—a great advantage to a trading and colonizing state.

Spain also possessed a poor section, the mountainous country on the Bay of Biscay. This remote and insignificant area was devoted to sea fishing, whereas the focus of Spanish economic interest was traditionally upon the interior plateau, a dry country given over to grazing and metal mining, with some dry-farming of wheat and

barley. The great advantage of both Spain and Portugal for overseas ventures was the centralized government each had evolved.
Centuries of fighting the Moors had forced every Iberian Christian
state of the northern mountains to subordinate all individual freedom to the church and the army. The resources of the succession
countries when they entered the contest for overseas trade and
empire were therefore completely under the control of their rulers.
They made up in unified effort a part of what they lacked in
resources because of the poverty of their homelands.

The Netherlands had an area not much larger than Denmark or
Portugal. It was a fishing country, but it had lush pastures also,
and its external and internal interests were about evenly balanced.
It occupied the mouth of the most active commercial waterway
in Europe, and the towns of this lowland were the leading handicraft centers north of the Alps. Thus it fell heir to much of the Hanseatic trade (Fig. 6, p. 36). As the natural coastal outlet of a large
fraction of Central Europe, it lay in the path of trade as soon as
the trans-Alpine routes were eclipsed by the ocean way to the
Orient. Its permanent handicaps were its small size and its land
frontier which was nothing more formidable than sand barrens
interspersed with peat bogs.

France, besides sharing in every advantage of its continental com-
petitors, was the largest and richest country in Europe. It had numerous harbors facing the Atlantic, many of which were the home
ports of daring fishermen. It had easy connections with the Rhine
trade-route. For good measure it controlled a reach of Mediterranean coast. It was not much farther from the Orient than Iberia,
and lay nearer to America. It possessed much fertile farmland,
diverse in climate, a fair number of towns, and a government which
was rapidly becoming centralized. It entered the colonial contest
late, partly because the unification of so large and varied a region
was a herculean task, and partly because, like the Netherlands, it
had a weak boundary toward Central Europe. The need to protect
that frontier has perennially sapped a considerable part of the
energy of France.

The British Isles were, like Norway, on the remote frontier,
so long as the axes of trade lay across the Alps and along the Rhine
and Rhône. Farther north than France, these islands held nothing
of its agricultural variety. They were mainly lowlands and fertile

[88]

enough to make farming the dominant interest of the small population. Sheep raising was the leading business. Owing to centuries of freedom from invasion, government had progressed in the direction of localism and individual liberty somewhat at the expense of centralized authority. Indeed the four nationalities of the two major islands were not amalgamated, and had traditionally been independent sovereignties. The fifteenth century showed an unpromising foundation for the cornerstone of the later British Empire. Yet, advantages for overseas trade there were. Plenty of ample harbors were evenly spaced about the major island. The agricultural base was adequate to supply a greatly increased population with staple food. Fishing was a significant supplementary means of livelihood. The habit of trade was already in being, because shipping wool to Flanders across the "narrow seas" had become a thriving business. Insularity guaranteed defense of the borders, provided an adequate navy was maintained. Naval vessels could readily be manned from the fishing fleets which worked out of every harbor on the islands. In a day when water transport was far better developed than overland transport, Britain, no less than the Netherlands, and more effectually than France, lay on the route between the mainland heart of European trade and handicrafts and the continents overseas. Freedom from wars gave English entrepôt ports along the Channel and the North Sea a long-run advantage over Holland and France in a day when water travel was greatly preferred to land transport. Finally, the government, peculiarly responsive as it was to local and bourgeois opinion, was liberal enough to favor new enterprises, such as those of "merchant adventurers" to the far corners of the earth.

EUROPE AND THE LARGER WORLD

As a result of embarking upon territorial extension by land and discoveries of new continents overseas, Europe pursued a course of trade, conquest, and colonization that swiftly brought its national states to a pinnacle of power over all the continents. Only a little less quickly, Europeans peopled all the middle-latitude lands not already fully occupied, while also increasing their home population many fold.

The early modern period of European history belonged to the Atlantic margin of the continent. There lay the states which had achieved the internal organization needed for operations on a large scale in the new world being discovered. They could now channel into national programs the vigor, imagination, and ruthlessness that earlier had been spent in internal turmoil. Their numerous harbors on the world ocean gave them the inducement to direct a part of their new-found energy overseas.

The reinforcement of strength drawn from overseas connections was used in large part to build colonial empires. Much later some of these distant foundations became powerful rivals of their European prototypes. Few events have been so momentous as Europe's identification of itself with the larger world of the six continents.

CHAPTER IV

Europe on the Threshold of The Industrial Revolution

A DECISIVE TURNING POINT IN MODERN
EUROPEAN HISTORY AND CULTURE

By tradition and common consent, the history of the Western world has been divided for convenience into three periods: Ancient, from the beginnings to the later fifth century A.D.; Medieval, to the mid-fifteenth century; Modern, to the present time. The transition from each age to the next was marked by a notable change in the distribution of settlement and the use of the earth's natural resources. These shifts in the relations between Europe and its inhabitants have been the subjects of the three preceding sections of this study. The five hundred years embraced in the Modern Age were punctuated, toward the end of the eighteenth century, by new uses of earth resources so comprehensive and extensive that they must be discussed in any treatment of the environmental foundations of European history. These changes are collectively known as the Industrial Revolution. It lagged behind the Agricultural and Commercial revolutions that ushered in the modern era, but when it came, reinforced them so vigorously that it set in motion a new sub-period of history.

The transmutation associated with the Industrial Revolution was initiated during two generations (*ca.* 1760-1825). At that time every aspect of European life—political, economic, social, and intellectual—was realigned to take account of the freshly utilized European environment that underlay the change. The movement spread from north to south and from west to east. Before it had gone far in the continent of its origin, it took hold in North America. Later it touched most countries of Europe and finally traced its lineaments on parts of every continent.

The depth and reach of the change warrant taking careful stock of the natural conditions discovered or exploited in new ways at the outset of the period, for it was then that the meager base of ancient and medieval techniques began its swift enlargement to the scale familiar in modern technology.

FORERUNNERS OF THE INDUSTRIAL REVOLUTION

The genesis of the transformation can be traced back to the end of the Middle Ages when the Revival of Learning marked a shift in man's thoughts from medieval otherworldliness and traditional dependence upon clerical direction, to humanism, individualism, and mundane goals. This refocusing of interest was reflected in the Age of Discoveries when rapid expansion of the known world and increasing mastery of the natural environment engrossed the attention of Europeans. European enterprise in making the Discoveries linked the seacoasts of the globe into a single thoroughfare, the highway of the sailing ship. In time Europe lost its ancient self-sufficiency, and became but one of six continents and—next to Australia—the smallest.

Despite this change in status, Europe maintained its initial advantage by further exploration of the other continents, by occupation of vast overseas territory, and by an ever-growing ocean-borne trade. The world was gradually transformed into an economic whole, if not into an economic unit, as commerce and colonization drew the natural resources of all the continents into a single system of exploitation. Europe led in this unprecedented integration of scattered mineral deposits, contrasting climates, and divergent technological skills, and profited hugely by the resulting advance in human productivity.

Technological Progress

Trade was the first activity to prosper, as the original trickle of luxury goods from the ancient civilization of the Orient swelled steadily in volume and variety, and frontier goods from beyond the Baltic mingled in European markets with the unfamiliar products of new frontier continents—Africa and the Americas. Almost at once the European trade sphere embraced the whole range of climates, and the distinctive products of every major population group of the globe.

Europe is ideally placed to profit by seaborne world-trade. The land surface of the earth (from which all but a negligible fraction of the earth's production is derived), is unequally distributed over the globe. If a great circle be drawn to include the maximum land area, the resultant hemisphere will be found to have its pole in the southern North Sea. Except for the obstacle offered to navigation by the Arctic ice directly north of this center, the ocean stretches uninterrupted in every direction to all the lands of the earth. The initiative of western Europeans in exploiting the possibilities of this universal water highway, gave the original impetus to the Commercial Revolution and, profiting from location in the middle of the land hemisphere, fixed the center of world trade in Atlantic Europe.

Practically all the arable and pastoral acreage of the earth likewise lies within the land hemisphere just described, or adjacent to it on extensions of the ocean trade routes that run in every direction from its European pole near the mouths of the Thames and the Rhine. Increased trade favored increased agricultural production of familiar kinds in Europe. Livestock and crop plants were also carried from one continent to another. In this process some new plants and animals, introduced into Europe, could be acclimated and they became useful additions to the regional economy of their new habitat. A larger number were unsuited to the European climate, but came to be commercially grown in lower latitudes on other continents to produce food, clothing, and many other goods useful to Europeans. In time the indigenous staples of each continent came to be raised in all suitable habitats of the earth. Today every staple crop and domestic beast has a range essentially coterminous with the habitat in which it can thrive. Europe has learned how to profit from the progress of this expansion by exploiting the vast acreages of the newly-won continents. Eventually mass production increased the supply of goods many fold; but until the full tide of the Industrial Revolution, the complete agricultural and commercial potential of the overseas world could not be realized.

[93]

Organizational Change

Technological progress in the use of earth resources took effect largely in the sphere of "political economy." An equally vital change occurred in the organization of society.

The profound religious revolution which goes by the name of the Protestant Reformation touched the lives of nearly all Europeans and changed the outlook of those who adopted the reformed faiths. The medieval ideal of a universe ordained and dominated by divine force, reflected on earth in dual world states, the Holy Roman Church and the Holy Roman Empire, was supplanted by a looser social order in which the individual assumed responsibility for personal acts. By extension, groups of individuals might organize politically into states, each assuming responsibility for its sovereign acts. The church either became an arm of such a state or it was completely separated from the political facet of the social order.

Thus the traditional idea of an amorphous world-state receded before a new conception, the national state. Within this novel political frame, the individual began to function in a new kind of world; the hitherto insignificant dwellers in towns, the bourgeoisie, rose swiftly to power; and eventually a different socio-economic doctrine, *laissez-faire*, appeared. The logic of these developments is clear, and it is no accident that the Treaty of Westphalia of 1648, which closed the bloodiest of religious wars, established also the implicit "right" of the individual to worship as national opinion (expressed by the national state) decided, rather than by decree of the universal church. This treaty recognized the legal existence of two essentially democratic commonwealths, Holland and Switzerland. In subsequent centuries industrial expansion was to be increasingly sponsored by national states. Their governments, feeling no preoccupation with the other world and unhampered by medieval tradition, were free to concentrate on exploiting the wealth of the segments of the earth which they severally controlled, be they inside or outside Europe.

Rulers of the national states vied with each other in governing according to canons expressed by the term "enlightenment." They patronized the arts and sciences, and sought the welfare of their subjects, down to the humblest. Nevertheless they remained despots,

[94]

however benevolent, and vigorously suppressed every evidence of popular movements that appeared along with the diffusion of material prosperity among the new bourgeoisie, and the lesser, but still noticeable improvement in the lot of lowlier classes.

Thanks to this far reaching change of outlook, individuals, released from religious restrictions as perhaps never before in history, and urged by fresh interest in an expanding world, felt free to investigate natural phenomena. Knowledge of remote lands unlike Europe, notable advances in mathematics, and the first steps in experimentation led to the birth of modern science and invention as the Reformation receded into the past. Practical solutions of the problems set by nature and advances in the theoretical knowledge of the material world gave men increasing skill in modifying their environment, and led to discoveries and inventions that brought about the Industrial Revolution.

THE ENVIRONMENTAL SETTING

The ferment of ideas and activities associated with the Renaissance and the Reformation diversified the thinking and expanded the economy of traditional Europe (*i.e.*, Europe as so far defined by history and habitat). The balance between its three major parts shifted, and territory was added and subtracted along its southern and eastern margins. To the eastward, Russia faced about from east to west and assumed a thin veneer of European culture under coercion by "enlightened despotism." In the south, the seesaw between Christian and Moslem societies continued.

An Unsettled Mediterranean

Mediterranean Europe retained its ineradicable natural distinctiveness, but lost both area and influence during the period embraced by the Discoveries and the Industrial Revolution.

The entire Eastern Basin was forfeited to the Turks, who successively invaded Asia Minor, the Balkan Peninsula, and the lower and middle basins of the Danube. On that side the border of Europe was retracted to the Adriatic Sea and the Danubian lands that could be held from a base at Vienna, located in a defensible pocket of mountains at the west edge of the grassy plains of southeastern Europe (Fig. 11, p. 96). The reduction in territory synchronized with the discovery of oceanic routes to the Orient, and new con-

FIG. 11. EASTWARD EXPANSION OF EUROPE

AND WESTWARD EXPANSION OF RUSSIA.

tinental outlets for European energy. Indeed the incursion of nomadic peoples from the grasslands of interior Asia (Fig. 2, p. 6) to block the Eastern Mediterranean trade connections had done more than anything else to instigate the Discoveries.

As European power shrivelled in the southeast, the westernmost Mediterranean peninsula, Iberia, took the leadership of Europe by expelling its Moslem rulers and the Levantine culture they had imposed, and prosecuting the sea voyages that resulted in opening the world seaway and the "new" continents.

Iberia was by environment and tradition part of the Mediterranean world. At the same time several of its harbors opened on the Atlantic; this gave the Spaniards and Portuguese opportunity to lead the overseas expansion that signalized modern history, and a chance to make immediate profits from initiating colonial enterprise. As decades passed, other Atlantic states entered the competition, and wrested larger and larger shares of overseas commerce from the Iberian pioneers. Nevertheless, until industrialization profoundly altered the relative values of natural resources, the Iberian states were rightly regarded as Great Powers. These national states derived no part of their newfound political weight from their Mediterranean habitat. Their power was based on control of overseas trade and colonies. This became clear when they relapsed into minor Mediterranean states upon losing their empires.

At the moment when the Balkan Peninsula was subjected to conquest from Asia, and the Iberian Peninsula turned its back on the Mediterranean world to face the overseas continents, the intervening Mediterranean coast of Europe entered its eclipse. Restricted to little more than the peninsula of Italy, this coast was cut off from commerce of the first magnitude, the primary basis of its former prosperity. The Italian contribution to trans-Alpine trade dwindled to local products, but these were still valuable enough to keep every section of the peninsula a pawn on the chessboard of the continental European powers—Spain, France, and Austria. In this period of political fragmentation and impotence, the Italian core of the Mediterranean world resembled North Central Europe more than any other part of the continent.

North Central Europe

In Central Europe north of the Alps, political fragmentation and loss of trade was nearly as widespread as in Italy, and within the original Holy Roman Empire of the German people perhaps more disastrous. There the area that had once pretended to inherit Rome's world-state had fallen apart to become "The Germanies" —more than 300 political units of diverse size, but all small. The Empire of which they were legally the parts could no longer control them; but neither could they exercise individual independence, because at one time or another most of them were in pawn to more powerful neighbors on the west and the east. Frequently their territory was overrun by armies of these rivals for European hegemony.

Subverted politically, this section had made little or no economic advance since the Middle Ages. Its commerce had actually diminished when, like Italy, it lost its cross-continent trade in oriental goods to countries on the Atlantic seaboard. Local and trans-Alpine commerce languished under the levies exacted by petty rulers of many tiny states through which goods had to pass.

East of the frontier of the ancient core of Germanic Europe (*i.e.*, along the Elbe and Saale rivers and the Bohemian Forest [Fig. 11, p. 96]), new and larger states had grown up during the later medieval and early modern eras (Fig. 8, p. 66). Two of them, Austria and Prussia, had begun within the fold of the Empire, but had incorporated territory beyond the farthest imperial confines. A third, Poland, mainly in the basin of the Vistula River, lay wholly outside imperial Europe. Together the new states added to North Central Europe at least twice as much territory as the older, strictly German part, had covered. Austria was in process of expansion down the Danube, with boundaries along the mountain borders of basins traversed by the middle course of that stream. Poland and Prussia were contenders for segments of the North European Plain, a lowland with only minor barriers usable for political boundaries—mainly marshes and forests likely to vanish with settlement of the land by farmers. Each of these frontier states included more than one language group, resembling in this respect the Atlantic states at a comparable stage of their evolution. Both appeared to be achieving national unity after the pattern established by France, Great Britain, and Spain. No one could have foreseen the subsequent failure of these states to complete the task of integrating the peoples of the land units to which they laid claim.

"Russia in Europe"

Still farther east, where the plain expands to continental size, other Slavic states grew up, mainly in the edge of the forest (Fig. 11, p. 96). Of these, Muscovy became dominant successively as the Russian Empire and the Soviet Union, and has expanded to occupy the vast core of the Eurasian continent.

In making its territorial growth, the original Muscovite state spread from a center at Moscow, near the water parting of streams flowing to the Baltic, Black, Caspian, and White Seas. During the early decades of modern European history, Russia made territorial accretions by pushing downstream toward all these seas. In the early seventeenth century, territory touching the Baltic Sea was reached and a hundred years later formally annexed, thus opening Russia's first "window to the West," *i.e.*, toward the Atlantic sea routes. By the end of the eighteenth century, a push across the plain had incorporated much of Poland. At about the same time the Turks were thrust back from the north shore of the Black Sea. This opened a second window toward the west, but it afforded no real connection, because the Turks continued to hold the outlet of the Black Sea into the Mediterranean. These acquisitions established Russian authority in lands that had been generally considered a part of Europe since the later Middle Ages. Territorial conquest was followed by active participation in European politics, and Russia began to make itself one of the states thought of as European. The commonly accepted eastern boundary of Europe came to be the line of the Ural Mountains and the Ural River, and old atlases separate "Russia in Europe" from "Russia in Asia" along that line. The distinction appears never to have been valid. The Russian governments until 1480 were dependencies of a power that had its seat in Central Asia, and Asiatic nomads occupied land well west of the Ural River until the mid-eighteenth century. Conversely, independent Muscovy pushed across the low passes of the Ural Mountains a century and a half before it overran the Baltic states, and reached the Pacific Ocean 84 years before the Baltic conquest was completed (Fig. 2, p. 6).

By contrast with this rapid march eastward, Russian absorption of its western conquests was a slow, piecemeal operation, steadfastly contested to the present moment. The eastern boundary of Europe appears to lie either in Russia's fluctuating western frontier zone or on the Pacific Ocean. Geography repudiates the claim for the narrow, low, and easily traversed Ural range because it never has served as a boundary, even for local administration inside the Russian state.

Beginning with its first seizure of Baltic frontage, Russian influence in European politics has been based chiefly on its overwhelming size and on the lack of natural barriers toward the much smaller states of East Central Europe. In the cultural and political movements from the revival of classical learning to the rise of natural science, Russia took no part, for during that period the Russian state was isolated from Europe.

At the time of the Discoveries, the Russians were a land-locked folk, professing the Greek Orthodox faith. Untouched by the Renaissance and Reformation, they reflected the Commercial Revolution in their expanding trade; but this traffic, thanks to the frontier nature of most of the country, was more akin to trade between Europe and the overseas continents than to European internal commerce. Exports consisted mainly of extractive goods—furs, timber, and beeswax. Russia likewise remained long unaware of the Agricultural Revolution which was revitalizing the exploitation of rural land in Europe proper. Legal serfdom survived until after the middle of the nineteenth century, and the three-field system was not abandoned until the Bolshevik Revolution that followed World War I.

After the Industrial Revolution had swept Western and Central Europe, grasslands of south Russia were converted from open range for livestock into wheat fields (Fig. 11, p. 96). This change only served to emphasize the non-European character of the country, because the same transformation was taking place in the overseas frontier continents, wherever similar conditions of soil and climate prevailed. During the nineteenth century every such region, including the sub-humid, black-soil region of Russia, began to grow wheat extensively to provide food for the urban population of Western and Central Europe.

The Industrial Revolution became effective in Russia only after the Soviet Republic supplanted the Czarist Empire. Its progress may be presumed to be shaping Russian economy to the pattern earlier worked out in Western Europe. At the same time the Soviet Russian political and social organization appears to differ more sharply from that of Europe than at any time since Muscovy began to imitate the West.

The Atlantic Seaboard

What Italy and Germany lost by the Discoveries was gained many times over by the seaboard states on the Atlantic front of the continent. The stimulus of overseas trade was first felt in Portugal, whence it made swift headway along the coast northward to Norway and Sweden.

Each of the states in this group had already been welded into a nation by centuries of joint endeavor, and had substituted internal unity for the minute subdivision of feudal tradition. Freed from internal strife, they were ready to embark upon enterprises beyond their own borders. Well-established central authority took prompt advantage of the commercial opportunities that were opened by explorations of other continents. After decades of trafficking and colonizing, Portugal, Spain, France, the Netherlands, and Britain held rich lands overseas, and Denmark and Sweden had small possessions and trading stations.

These Atlantic seaboard countries sent to the overseas continents cloth, pottery, hardware, ornaments, and other products of handicraft. They received in return foodstuffs, beverages, raw materials for the craftsman, and (from East and South Asia) silks, lacquers, jades, and other luxury goods. The larger part of the profits went into the pockets of European merchants, who were the entrepreneurs, middlemen, and owners of the ships in which the goods were carried.

THE TRANSPORT PATTERN

Seaports

Ocean-going ships were not large, and could put into shallow harbors. The whole Atlantic coastline of Europe has been drowned beneath the sea in recent geological times. In the process salt water has run up all the river valleys and other low-lying lands facing the ocean, converting them into estuaries and bays, some of which penetrate the shoreline sixty miles or more. Because it is cheaper to carry goods by sea than by land, the heads of long estuaries were especially favored as sites for seaports (Fig. 8, p. 66). Provided the approach was wide enough for easy sailing, coasting vessels and, later, transoceanic ships could make these harbors their terminals. Amsterdam, Antwerp, Bordeaux, Bristol, Lisbon, and London are conspicuous examples of such ports. There are many similar sites, only a little less desirable. These gave rise to ports serving local hinterlands. By the mid-eighteenth century, the whole coast from Cadiz to Bergen teemed with busy harbors.

Inland Transport

Rivers were the chief inland highways, and the collection and distribution of goods for overseas trade was easiest where inland waters could be used. Most of the large streams flow into broad estuaries. Port towns at the head of tidewater on navigable streams were further enlivened by river craft.

Europe is highly favored in the number of separate navigable rivers that flow directly into the sea, rather than combining into a single system, like that of the Mississippi. Even so, the rivers are not close enough together to provide a complete natural network of waterways, and have come to be supplemented by canals wherever possible. On the flat but narrow coastal plain, and particularly on the broader Rhine-Scheldt delta, canal building without flights of locks was possible. There, single locks were used as early as the fourteenth century, chiefly to move from tidal streams to fresh-water canals. Navigation canals in sloping country required steps of locks, and a constant supply of water to operate them. This more intricate form of canal was in use before the end of the seventeenth century (Table 1, p. 104).

Where streams were lacking or so swift that engineering was unequal to the task of providing canals, roads might be built at public expense to supplement the system of waterways.

By these means, established handicraft towns in the Atlantic countries were put in touch with the sea, and the larger market towns and provincial capitals were able to satisfy their less specialized but ever-growing wants without excessive charges for haulage. Thus the same seaboard nations which had had a favorable situation for building up colonial empires along with their colonial trade, were favored by nature with means of spreading the benefits of their economic and political expansion throughout their homelands.

Improvements in transportation were undertaken in Central Europe as well as in the seaboard countries, but they often lagged for want of money. To be worthwhile, canals and roads had to pass through a number of the tiny countries of this region. It proved difficult or impossible to get the small and mutually jealous governments to plan and construct a comprehensive route system. Hence, even where funds were available, few canals or roads were built.

In the coastal countries favored with overseas connections, there was room for further expansion of commerce, but it could come about only through reduction in the cost of export articles. Cheaper goods would widen the market among the numerous but, by European standards, very poor people of the overseas lands—especially Asia, Africa, and low-latitude America. Cheaper goods might be produced if the cost of transport could be further lowered, or if the cost of fabrication could be reduced.

TABLE 1

CHRONOLOGY OF CRITICAL ITEMS IN THE DAWN OF THE INDUSTRIAL REVOLUTION

Canal with flight of locks (Canal du Midi)—1681
Steam pump used in mines—1725
Flying shuttle for looms—1733
First use of coke for smelting iron—1735
Blast furnace fired with coke—1760
Canal with aqueduct (Worsley coal field to Manchester)—1761
Spinning jenney (worked by hand)—1764
Spinning frame (run by water power; originally by horse power)—1769
Steam engine (with condenser)—1769
Spinning mule (yarn for fine muslins)—1779
Steam piston power converted into rotary motion—1781
Steam powered spinning machine—1785
Power (water power) loom—1785
Puddling and rolling iron—ca. 1785
Cotton gin—1793
High pressure steam engine—ca. 1800
Steam towage on canals (Forth & Clyde Canal)—1802
Steamship—1815
Machines wholly of iron and steel—ca. 1820
Steam railroad (Darlington)—1825

The *Canal du Midi* (Table 1, above) carried barges across southern France between the Mediterranean and the Atlantic. This canal, equipped with the first long flight of locks, was a major innovation in inland navigation, and was soon followed by others in France, the Low Countries, and Great Britain. It was nearly a century before a canal was carried across a stream in an aqueduct, thus beginning the partial emancipation of navigation from local streams. Further outstanding improvements in internal waterways had to await the application of power through machinery, steam towage being an example.

Roads are somewhat less costly to construct than canals. Nevertheless in humid Western Europe, where streams are numerous and rains are frequent, the combined expense of bridge- and road-building and of maintenance was high. A more serious handicap was costliness of operation, which limited their use to passengers, mails, and the most valuable freight. Areas that could be tapped only by roads remained out of easy touch with the world until the advent of the steam "railroad" at the end of the first phase of the Industrial Revolution (Table 1, p. 104).

NEW APPLICATIONS OF POWER

The most direct means of lowering the cost of fabricating goods, was to substitute machines for hand operations. Even the simplest tools are machines of a sort, but until the modern era few changes in tools had been made since classical times.

Animate Power

Of the principal commodities made for the export trade, textiles lent themselves most readily to mechanical fabrication. In a few instances, simple machines (*e. g.*, spinning wheels and looms) had long since replaced hand labor, and reduction in cost of production had been effected. For example, the loom operated by hands and feet was faster, and its output was more uniform than textiles woven on a primitive hand loom. Machines of this sort continued to be invented, but they soon outran the feeble physical power of human muscle, and even that of animals (on treadmills and turntables), and so were useless. Want of mechanical power was clearly the decisive bar that limited progress toward larger output and lower costs.

In none of its many aspects did the Industrial Revolution stamp so conspicuous a mark on human society as by broadening the base and increasing the scope of mechanical power.

[105]

Inanimate Power

Europeans of the early eighteenth century were familiar with small jobs of harnessing fragments of the tremendous power residing in natural forces. Brooks tumbling down hillsides or dropping over rock bars were dammed to divert a part of their flow to huge and cumbersome water wheels, which turned millstones for grinding grist or ran saws for making lumber. Along the deeply indented coasts of North Europe, where the ebb and flow of the tide ranges between 15 and 30 feet, small tidemills were run by salt water. In districts lacking water power, people built wide-armed windmills on exposed hills all over Europe, and on flat ground along the windy Atlantic and North Sea coasts. In most places these were gristmills or sawmills, but on the wet delta of the Rhine, and in lesser wet flats in other rainy parts of the continent, windmills pumped surplus water off pastures and fields, and so added farmlands high in value and not inconsiderable in quantity to the continent's usable acreage.

Each of these small-scale applications of power suffered the inherent handicap of unreliability. Low water forced mills to cease operations; spring freshets carried unwelcome sand and gravel into the mill pond and sometimes burst the dam. Tidemills could operate only while the tide was strongly ebbing, i. e., considerably less than half the time and often at inconvenient hours. Windmills stopped when the wind fell off, as it frequently and unpredictably did in European latitudes.

Besides these limitations, windmills and tidemills could not be enlarged to increase their individual output of power, which was invariably small. In contrast, many large streams were broken by falls and rapids, and were capable of furnishing much power. Unluckily, such power sites were generally in mountainous or hilly country with sparse populations poor in resources and unused to machinery.

Power from Falling Water. Harnessing of the larger streams nevertheless marked one starting point of the Industrial Revolution. Such streams furnished concentrated blocks of power far larger than the brooks hitherto used. Their flow was reasonably reliable throughout the driest season, because they were fed by a large watershed.

The streams of Northwest Europe were more readily usable at this stage of technology than those of other sections of the continent. The long, rainless summer of the Mediterranean climate reduces even the major rivers to a small fraction of their winter flow. Rivers fed by melting Alpine snowfields and glaciers are no steadier, because they run full in summer and diminish greatly during the snowbound winter. In Central Europe, cold winters regularly seal the streams with ice, and so reduce their flow; frequent, but unpredictable rains or sudden thaws cause floods. In the Northwest where snow and ice are light, summer evaporation at a minimum, and rainfall evenly distributed, the stream flow is fairly even all the year round, with slight risk of violent stoppage or damage of waterworks.

Within each of the three climatic regions, the streams most amenable to the inexpert techniques of the middle eighteenth century flowed through hill-lands, rather than mountains. The great power inherent in the long leaps of torrents in glaciated mountains such as the Alps, Pyrenees, or Scandinavian ranges could be utilized only by costly, large-scale engineering which lay beyond the capacity of the pioneers in industrialization.

On this basis, the most favored areas for advances in water-power exploitation were the hilly core of the Island of Britain, the Ardennes, and other hills of the lower Rhine country, and the northwest, rain-facing slopes of the *Massif Central* of France. Among these regions, the French and the British areas had the further advantage of belonging to political units well advanced in overseas commerce and colonial expansion. They owed their superiority in world trade largely to their location on the margin of Europe, which brought their long coastal frontages close to the center of the land hemisphere.

For some time France and Britain made approximately equal strides toward more effective utilization of water-power from their larger streams. Then Britain drew ahead. Insular security permitted British businessmen uninterrupted experimentation with machinery and expansion of colonial business, whereas French efforts were repeatedly distracted by military struggles on the landward frontier and repressed by a government intent on integrating all the nation's forces.

The harnessing of water-power on a moderately large scale after centuries of letting it run to waste, reflects the impact of two separate lines of influence: the progress of science and invention dating from the Revival of Learning and tending toward increased mastery of the local natural environment; the expansion into new worlds having fresh natural resources, begun during the Discoveries and accentuated by commerce. Inventors set themselves to keep pace with the growing possibilities for trade by manifolding the productivity of European labor through mechanical contrivances.

Textile Manufacture. One of the commonest commodities in trade has always been cloth, and the textile trade was one of the first to respond to the new forces. Florence, the cities of Flanders, and seaports the world over had prospered for centuries by making or trading in textiles. The extent and antiquity of this commerce is suggested by the fact that some fifty towns have given their names to various kinds of cloth. The long-established but small trade in woolens and linens handloomed in Europe, silks made in the Far East, and cottons in India was redoubled as decreasing costs of transportation, made possible by the new ocean trade routes, lowered prices, and so increased the demand for all sorts of textiles. Invention of machines to spin yarn and weave fabrics promised still further reduction in costs of production, but water-power to run these machines was not available on the lowlands where most of Europe's population lived, though it ran to waste in the hills.

Sylvan streams throughout Northwest Europe saw the rapid establishment of chains of towns on their banks, wherever there were suitable sites for dams. Factories soon absorbed the small labor supply available from sparse local populations, and began to draw upon more remote districts. Whole families migrated from distant towns and countryside, attracted by year-round jobs provided by perennial water-power. The movement calls attention to one of the most striking aspects of the Industrial Revolution, *viz.*, the rearrangement of the pattern of population. There was both a pronounced overall increase, and a shift from rural to preponderantly urban character. Towns grew up where none previously existed, while old centers languished as traditional market-town business was diverted to burgeoning factory cities.

The manufacture of textiles introduced several applications of large-scale mechanical power that later spread to other industries, notably metal- and wood-working (Table 1, p. 104). Before long, factories were set up to make the machines used to fabricate consumer goods.

The less bulky raw materials followed cotton, woolen, and the other fibers to the water-power sites. Bulky or heavy materials might fail to repay the cost of overland transportation. For them, and subsequently for all sorts of factory output, a novel source of power was made available. This was water in the form of its vapor, steam.

Coal, and Steam Power. Like the power of falling water, the force of steam had long been known. But no application of steam power had been attempted until the time of the Industrial Revolution. The first workable steam engine invented was designed to pump excess ground water from a mine. The up-and-down motion of pumping was essentially that of the piston of the engine, working back and forth in its cylinder. Pumps could also be operated by water-power, but few power sites were found conveniently overlying wet mines.

Steam power is more mobile. It can be generated by burning any combustible. Wood was the most obvious fuel in Northwest Europe, but it was already growing scarce, with increasing population and consumption for heat, cooking, and smelting iron. The voracious boiler of a stationary engine soon depleted the woodland within hauling radius, and necessity rather than chance dictated that the first successful steam engine should be fired by coal, the fuel being drawn from the very mine it kept dry.

Owing to the high concentration of heat in coal, steam engines pumping out the mines consumed only a tiny fraction of the coal brought to the surface. At the same time, every improvement in steam engines increased the available power from each ton of coal. This could be used to run all sorts of machines, and factory towns could be built on coal fields as well as beside water-power (Fig. 12, p. 110). Indeed, a small area underlaid by thick coal seams can support a steam-powered industrial development many times more intensive than can any but the most exceptional water-power site, and without risking imminent exhaustion of the fuel.

Where coal lies close to the seacoast or on a navigable stream, it can be cheaply transported to other districts, thus enhancing the mobility of power produced from it. The proximity of a few coal fields to navigable water made them early centers of export.

FIG. 12. COAL AND IRON ORE

MINOR AND LOW-GRADE

DEPOSITS OF EUROPE.

DEPOSITS ARE NOT SHOWN.

Much of the coal sent out was used in steamships, rather than in factories. Whether on waterways or not, most fields producing coal especially suitable for making steam became the sites of mill towns. Factories on the coal fields vied with factories on water-power sites in the race for preëminence in output of machine-made goods.

With the rise of coal as a motive power, Britain further out-distanced France, because France had little coal, and all but a small fraction of it lay along the Belgian border, where wars raged during the formative years of the Industrial Revolution. In peaceful Britain, coal was abundant, of high grade, and widely distributed.

Coal stepped the dawning machine age up to a new level of production, and today, after two centuries and despite technical advances in using other forms of energy, it remains by all odds the chief source of mechanical power. Indeed, no combination of power sources at present available can compete with coal in total energy produced. Despite this preponderant position, it is another use of coal that has turned out to be its special contribution to the modern industrial world. While steam power generated by coal lowered prices of manufactures and transformed rural landscapes into cities, minerals and combinations of minerals smelted over coal-coke completed the foundations of a new material civilization, the age of steel.

NEW USES OF MINERALS

Minerals constitute one of the five great groups of natural resources. Some of them have always been used by human societies, even the most primitive. The mineral dominantly employed for tools and weapons by any society has commonly given its name to the civilization of that society. The "stone age," the "bronze age," the "iron age," the "steel age" are familiar terms that bespeak the position of minerals and implements at the core of human progress throughout history.

Following this logic, the later decades of the modern era may properly be called the "multi-metal age," for during the last two centuries mankind has learned to use tools, machines, and weapons on a scale beyond the imagination of earlier epochs. In geographic terms this development has meant discovery of hundreds of new uses for old minerals, utilization of new minerals hitherto unknown or regarded as valueless, and an acceleration in the shifting of population. Minerals have generally been the earliest attraction to draw people into unsettled districts as new uses and new values have sent prospectors and miners all over the earth. Finds have usually been followed by the mushroom growth of mining camps, sometimes by permanent changes in the population.

The Marriage of Iron with Coal

The industrial age did not spring full-fledged into being, but grew slowly and painfully out of the searching minds and patient experiments of many men. At the outset no new minerals were brought into use, and only a few of the well-known ones were given new applications. Yet these changes were so basic that they revolutionized economic society. The leaders in this development were iron and coal.

Iron had already given humankind a boost some two thousand years earlier, when men learned to substitute iron tools and weapons for bronze or stone implements. Steel had been widely used for swords, cutlery, and numerous other items for many hundred years. Yet, until the latter part of the eighteenth century, the world output of both iron and steel remained small.

During all this time the forges were tiny and scattered. The simple metallurgy of those days could cope only with ores containing few or no refractory substances. Primitive mining was confined to the iron deposits that happened to lie close to the surface. Many such deposits exist, but they are small. The only known fuel for smelting the ore was charcoal, made by slow combustion of wood. To be assured a long life, an iron furnace had to stand in a heavily wooded district, and keep its output small. Otherwise it would before long exhaust the fuel supply within the profitable radius for hauling charcoal, a light but bulky commodity. Iron and steel goods were therefore made in small furnaces, scattered over districts where wood and ore lay close together.

The Mediterranean world, famous from Damascus to Toledo for fine steel, was hopelessly at a disadvantage in the matter of large-scale output. Its climate produced only scrub woodland, and centuries of cutting had long since reduced available wood to patches of brush in the hillier sections. Dense forests still covered much ground in Central and Eastern Europe, but these parts had hardly begun to feel the urge to develop manufacturing beyond crude and simple handicraft. Northwest Europe was the true birthplace of iron and steel production.

By 1700 wood for charcoal smelting was already beginning to run short in Northwest Europe, and some ironmasters experimented with coal. Most of these innovators lived in Great Britain, where there were numerous accessible deposits of coal. By charring coal, coke is produced, and this could be used in place of charcoal for smelting. Coal from some fields made a type of coke that proved unsatisfactory in the smelter; at other mines coke could be directly substituted for charcoal, with excellent results. At first no notable advance in technique was made, but before long, the substitution of coal as the smelting fuel completely metamorphosed both the geographic and the economic status of iron and steel production.

The Geographic Pattern of Iron and Steel Making. At once it became possible to increase the scale of production because a few square miles underlaid with coking coal promised to support a large furnace for decades, perhaps centuries. Steam pumps, run by coal, permitted deep mining of both coal and iron, and further extended the life of mines. Still, only a few coal fields could be used at all, however suitable their product for coking, because iron ore, heavy and bulky, could be economically transported only where navigable water was available to bear the burden. About Birmingham, England, coking coal and easily worked iron were found together. In a few other places, coal or iron, mined on the seashore or a navigable stream, benefitted from water transport. Such favored districts had initially a monopoly of large-scale iron and steel production.

The new and underdeveloped continents lacked both markets and labor, and this disadvantage postponed their industrialization, even in the rare districts possessing both ore and coking coal, such as Birmingham, Alabama. The old civilizations of East and South Asia had not benefited from the stimuli which were stirring inventive minds in Europe, and made no noteworthy advances in the industrial arts. Europe alone was intelligently and economically prepared to experiment. All parts of the continent west of Russia and Turkey stood at somewhat the same stage of technology.

Hence the districts where the two critical raw materials were found together, or could be cheaply brought together, were able to take the lead over their rivals.

A glance at a map of iron ore and coal (Fig. 12, p. 110) will show that the island of Britain was the only part of Europe in which large deposits of ore and coking coal lay side by side, or within a short and cheap haul by water, involving no crossing of political boundaries. England's position at the focus of the major ocean routes and its insular security from foreign wars, had already enabled it to take the lead in the Commercial Revolution, and in the concommitant acquisition of overseas colonies. England also possessed the most favored conditions for factories based on water-power, and was beginning to feel the need for cheap production of textile machinery. It would have been surprising indeed, if England, thus prepared for economic progress, had not taken the cue from nature and begun to pioneer in the smelting of iron ore with coke coal.

Subsequently, ore and coal, somewhat separated but lying adjacent to different parts of a river system, as in the Rhine Basin, were brought together by water transport. Steel districts have grown up on coal fields lacking ore, on iron ore bodies lacking coal, and at intervening points where routes favor breaking bulk or transfer from one form of carriage to another.

The use of water and coal for power, and of large supplies of cheap iron and steel, comprised the foundation on which the Industrial Revolution was built. From iron and steel were fabricated machines that made possible the factory system; railroads and ships that reduced the time and the cost of transport to a fraction of their former levels, and so permitted world-wide marketing of the products of the European factories; agricultural machinery that took the place of labor in the new continents and produced a steady flow of raw materials to European factories and of food to European laborers.

This sequence of events was a complicated one, involving new applications of power, inventions, large-scale output of many raw materials, old and new, amplifications of the Agricultural Revolution in Europe, its extension into the new continents, and an intricate interaction of all these elements upon each other and upon social and political life.

[115]

Supplementary Minerals

The fundamental character of coal and iron should blind no one to the fact that other minerals have played smaller but often decisive parts from the outset of the Industrial Revolution. With every advance in the art of metallurgy, and with successive discoveries of new uses for minerals, the base of industrialized society of the European type has broadened.

Within Europe, countries and regions possessing these lesser minerals have entered into the fellowship of industrial society. It should be emphasized, however, that the drawing power of coal, especially in conjunction with iron ore, sucks most of the secondary minerals from their scattered mines to established manufactural towns on the coal fields or in their vicinity. The same attraction draws minerals to Europe from the other continents, most notably where Europe is poor in a key resource, such as tin.

THE BALANCE OF EUROPE AND THE OTHER CONTINENTS

With every discovery of mineral wealth, both within and without Europe, the internal equilibrium of the continent and the economic balance between it and its potential rivals have trembled.

Any serious threat to European world-supremacy, however, lay beyond the horizon of the eighteenth century. At that time, thanks to its early start, fortunate location, and varied resources, the continent of Europe as a whole, the western seaboard states in particular, and Britain above all, were on the threshold of the most prosperous era of their history. No menace to this prosperity and this supremacy came clearly into view until the twentieth century had dawned.

CHAPTER V

Europe on the Threshold
of Tomorrow

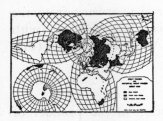 In the long view of thousand-year inter-
vals, European history falls short only
half a century of rounding out another
millennium. Just how much of the earth will be assigned to the
"European" part of western civilization in 2000 A D. is beyond
prediction, but some light can be thrown forward as a reflection
of present-day geography.

In the four preceding chapters, Europe has been presented on
the threshold of momentous changes that history has already
recorded. The outcome has guided the author in selecting the
aspects of geography that proved to be critically important in each
epoch. Turning to Europe on the threshold of tomorrow, he faces
an unknown future, without the invaluable aid of completed events
ranged in the perspective of elapsed time.

The easy course would omit any survey of contemporary natural
environment as the platform on which European life will be built
in the coming decades or centuries. A stable world would make it
both pointless and unnecessary to discuss further a habitat unchanged and promising a continuing and progressive unfolding
of European power along established lines. But a generation that
has struggled through two worldwide wars and sweeping, violent
changes in all aspects of European life, makes no assumption of
stability. It seems more likely that the present ferment is as por-

[117]

tentous as the flux which ushered in each earlier period of history. Earth resources are being put to uses, old and new, on a scale never before attained. Communication is escaping the lines along which it formerly moved, attached to the earth surface.

Critical alterations in the relations between mankind and its natural environment have been associated with each new period of Europe's history. The events of the next years cannot be forecast, but the trends in Europe's earth-setting can be surveyed by adopting the procedure that proved useful in the earlier chapters.

EUROPE AT THE END OF THREE MILLENNIA

In 1910 or thereabouts, most people would have conceded to Europe the entire peninsular area of Eurasia westward from the Ural Mountains, Ural River, and Caspian Sea, together with the Mediterranean shores of the Asian and African continents (Fig. 11, p. 96).

Europe about 1910

Thus inclusively pictured, Europe appears as the product of expansion from the eastern end of the Mediterranean—first westward, then northward, and finally eastward. This progression was punctuated by setbacks, especially the loss during several centuries of much of the Mediterranean world. Nevertheless, by the time World War I broke out, the African shoreline had once more been made politically subservient to European states and Turkey had adopted for the Asiatic seafront all the ways of the Occident except for religion.

In the course of widening the home base, Europe also proliferated by way of the oceans into all the continents. The European impress varied in depth and kind, from place to place. In the middle-latitude zones of every continent, climates may be found similar to those of Europe. To such kindred environments, transplanted Europeans introduced the material technology and social organization of their home continent. Wherever they found the indigenous population sparse, they settled in force, and the new European way of life took firm root. In regions where dense population and ancient and highly organized civilizations kept Europeans from settling in large numbers, businessmen tied the newly discovered lands into the expanding network of commerce, government officials administered key points, chiefly port cities, and missionaries undertook to modify the social order. Some of these countries imitated European practices in much detail, at least in superficial ways.

The low-latitude climates, generally not well suited to Europeans, were occupied by small groups of residents who employed native or other tropical races as the source of labor. In the very hot and wet lowlands the light-skinned intruders could do little more than "sit down in the country," without setting up permanent homes or founding families.

These variations in the depth of the European impress were somewhat masked by the uniformities of European organization. Out in front stood a political system of colonies grouped into empires headed by European states, and sovereign ex-colonies dominated by their European population and mode of life. Together, Europe and its associated territories covered much of the earth's land surface. Less visible but even more inclusive was economic interdependence that utilized the earth's resources more or less as a unit. A worldwide system of trade permitted large freedom in exchange of products, and to that extent favored the production of each kind of goods in the environment to which it was best suited by nature. Social customs and mental attitudes, rooted in different regions and reinforced by disparate histories, seemed less amenable to Europeanization than either political or economic life. Nevertheless, weighed in the balance in 1910 the worldwide diffusion of European government and trade tilted the scale heavily against regional particularism, in the view of careful observers in all parts of the world.

Effective political control of the interdependent economic world was seated firmly in Europe. Of the six states called "Great Powers," (Fig. 13, p. 120), three were European nations that had crystallized out of the Middle Ages centuries earlier. Two had been slower to slough off their feudal fragmentation, but once unified (a generation before) were in all respects European. One, Russia on the eastern fringe of Europe, had conquered considerable European territory and had faithfully imitated the European political structure and economic practices.

The Great Powers were supported by the lesser European states, several of which possessed valuable holdings overseas. Europe itself

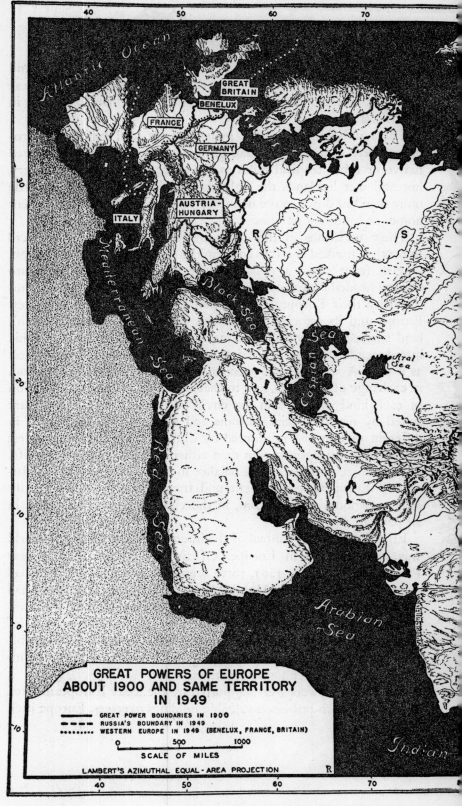

GREAT POWERS OF EUROPE
ABOUT 1900 AND SAME TERRITORY
IN 1949

——————— GREAT POWER BOUNDARIES IN 1900
— — — — RUSSIA'S BOUNDARY IN 1949
•••••••••• WESTERN EUROPE IN 1949 (BENELUX, FRANCE, BRITAIN)

0   500   1000
SCALE OF MILES

LAMBERT'S AZIMUTHAL EQUAL-AREA PROJECTION

FIG. 13. GREAT POWERS OF EUROPE

ABOUT 1900 AND THE SAME TERRITORY IN 1949.

incorporated by far the largest developed body of natural resources to be found in any one continent. With its overseas political empires and economic satellites, it appeared to be the center of gravity of a world held in unshakable equilibrium.

Portents of change, dating from the first decade of the nineteenth century, were hardly apparent to Europeans of that time. Two states remote from Europe displayed an expansive force that suggested promotion some day to the ranks of the Great Powers. The United States of America obtained colonies by depriving Spain of the remnants of its colonial empire. Japan waged a successful war against Russia and obtained a colonial outpost on the Asiatic mainland. But these budding powers either inherited or imitated the system established in Europe.

Europe about 1950

In a single generation stability gave place to mutation. Two successive wars, started in Europe by Europeans, spread along the tentacles of empire and the antennas of commerce to embroil all the other continents in combat, or at least to engage them in furnishing goods needed by the warring countries. The close of each conflict left Europe with cities in ruins, populations reduced, accumulated capital destroyed, foreign investments liquidated, and natural resources depleted. Indeed, neither war was ended until direct military aid was brought into the European theater of operations from other continents.

Great Power all but vanished from the European scene during the first half of the twentieth century (Fig. 13, p. 120). Dislocation of the seats of power began in the east.

At the end of World War I Austria was dismembered into minor states that have since been loosely grouped with the small neighboring nations between the German and Russian homelands. Their combined area has been called a "shatter belt," a term aptly characterizing its political geography. Even before the war was concluded, Russia had dropped out of the fighting, when its government was overthrown by internal turmoil. The consequent social revolution absorbed all Russian energy, and the state forfeited to the shatter belt the fringe of traditionally European lands which it had held by conquest for one to two centuries. By the end of hostilities Russia had ceased to participate in European affairs, withdrawing to its inland plain. Thereafter it depended upon itself, including its Asiatic heritage. Of the three eastern powers, Germany suffered least, but was deprived of its overseas colonies and some borderlands in Europe.

At the end of World War II the remaining European power centers were seen to be severely shaken. Germany was dismembered by military conquest which solidified into a political occupation. Italy was bereft of its colonies, and the inadequacy of its inherent resources as a base for a Great Power was confirmed. France was weakened by both wars, to what extent was not yet clear four years after it had been liberated from German occupation. If its power position has not waned in the absolute sense, it is lower in comparison to the post-war leaders.

Of the European Powers only Britain indisputably retains a position among the Greats. It is significant that a part of its strength flows from its colonies, and some of its vitality from the now autonomous countries overseas that remain joined with Great Britain and Northern Ireland in the Commonwealth of Nations (Fig. 14, p. 124).[1]

With minor exceptions, the lesser nations of Europe suffered from war as severely as did the Great Powers. The overall weakening of the continent was dramatically disclosed at the end of each conflict. Most visible was widespread damage to and, in places, utter destruction of the elaborate physical plant that had been created out of abundant and varied natural resources by many generations of human labor and intelligence. Less easily seen, but critical in a Europe needing quick rebuilding, was the loss by death of millions of people, and for the war years, by withdrawal of millions more from construction to destruction. Invisible but vital was the heavy drain on natural resources necessary to prosecute the wars. To it must be added the drafts required to restore the devastated areas.

The Europe of 1910 is generally acknowledged to have possessed a larger aggregation of natural resources, developed and potential, than any other continent. In a climate generally humid and mild, its moderately fertile soils had been improved by centuries of careful management. Soils unsuitable for crops or pasture were nearly

[1] The tendency of the British power center to shift from Great Britain appears in the decision in 1948 to eliminate from the designation "British Commonwealth of Nations" the adjective denoting its European origin.

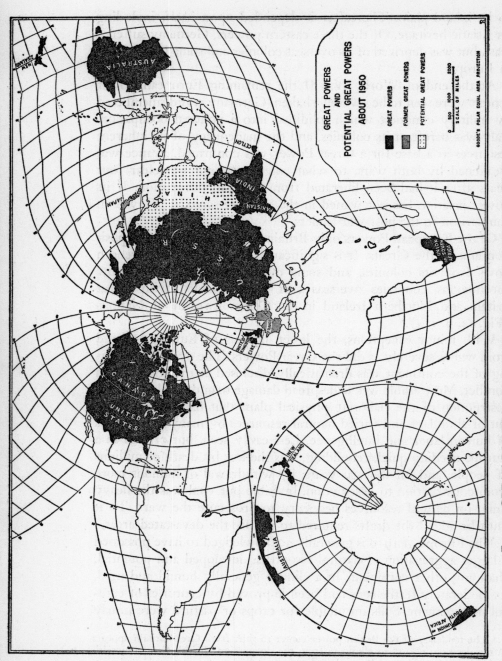

Fig. 14. GREAT POWERS AND POTENTIAL GREAT POWERS ABOUT 1950.

Areas in solid black, representing the United States of America, the Soviet Union, and the self-governing dominions of the (British) Commonwealth of Nations suggest the flight of

everywhere planted to forests. A large fraction of its widely distributed water-power was harnessed. Among its varied minerals coal and iron were abundant and widely distributed.

Using the surface resources as Europe had learned to do keeps them in balance or improves them. Thus, inventions between 1910 and 1950 reduced the cost of nitrate fertilizer for farmlands and extended the range of electric power. Minerals are in different case, because they are destroyed or depleted by use, no matter how wise and conservative. Europe's rich storehouse of minerals has long been heavily drawn upon by everyday needs because of dense population making its living by the manufacture of goods for export as well as home consumption.

Wars increase the draft on all natural resources, and upset balanced utilization. In Europe farms have been forced to produce wartime crops at the expense of the soil, and forests have been overcut. It will take time to restore them to pre-war productivity. Minerals have been recklessly consumed for armaments and munitions. Even though some new mines and even a few new minerals have been added to pre-war production, Europe today is so much poorer in total mineral resources than it was before 1914 that it has lost its long lead over other continents. Perhaps both North America and Asia outrank it in unused mineral wealth. For the time at least, North America is producing more goods than all of Europe combined. The deterioration in production is paralleled by the loss of political prestige. North America and Asia have not only increased their output of goods, they are also the seats of states which have grown to the stature of Great Powers while European Great Powers have declined or disappeared. Wars have hastened this shift in rank, but the underlying causes of both the wars and the demotion of European states must be sought in a profound change of the sort that historians recognize as the dawn of a new era.

EUROPE FACED WITH NON-EUROPEAN GREAT POWERS

Not one continental European state remains incontestably a Great Power, whereas the United States of America and the Union of Socialist Soviet Republics are widely acclaimed as the ranking Powers of today, with the Commonwealth of Nations, sprung from the British Islands, as a third (Fig. 14, opposite). It is noteworthy that all three of these states are by name and in fact unions or aggregations of territory. Each comprises vastly more area than is available to any existing continental European state. So wide is the disparity that each of the aggregations has a larger population, more varied climates, and greater diversity and quantity of natural resources than are available to even the best-endowed European states. The outstanding advantage of Europe, *viz.*, a habitat almost everywhere suited to dense settlement, is vitiated by political subdivision that diffuses the energy of its inhabitants. The three indisputable Great Powers include vast areas of slight productivity or valuable for only one or two reasons, but their populous and productive corelands are themselves large and diversified, judged by European standards. The outsize scale of non-European political units is a prime factor in assessing the position of Europe in the coming decades.

The Transport Revolution

The half century that has riveted mankind's attention to warmaking has been marked also by the culmination of a revolution in transport comparable only to the discovery of the world ocean, 400 years earlier. This is, of course, the use of the air as a medium of movement. By cutting the time needed for travel, and by eliminating the transfer between sea and land vehicles, the parts of the earth, including every political unit, have been brought closer together.

The process reaches back to improvements in transport made possible by steam power and cheap steel, and in that sense is a product of the Industrial Revolution. The steamship accelerated water transport and enabled ocean traffic to follow shortcuts denied to sailing vessels. A series of inventions made overland transport as comfortable as movement by water, and faster. First came the steam railroad, a contemporary of the steamship. Then petroleum in internal combustion engines rejuvenated the world's highways and began to supplant steam on railroads. In making the vehicles, aluminum and other light metals supplemented steel. When petroleum fuel was made to carry light metals aloft, maximum terrestrial speeds were left far behind, and transport was possible from point to point on the earth surface, rather than along lines traced on the ground or the sea.

[126]

All three of the states conceded to be Great Powers at the end of World War II had taken form during the decades when faster sea and land transport were increasing the radius of human action many fold. By the time air transport combined with its predecessors to make possible the contemporary transport system, these states were large and unified enough to benefit from the faster internal communication by air.

The Frame of Europe's Political Pattern

Very different was the setting in which the European Great Powers were shaped, and the tempo of the world in which they took the leadership was much slower. The political pattern which Europe has retained to the middle nineteen hundreds took shape much earlier, in an era when farming was the dominant business and trade was restricted to the slow movement of boats sailed or rowed on rivers and along coasts, and of horses and asses toiling along trails and unpaved roads. Nearly all the states remained tiny, because only those most favored by both nature and events were able to amass much territory. Great Britain, France, and Spain emerged into the Modern period of history as nations ranking large among their European neighbors. They profited greatly from the Discoveries, and maintained their position as the Great Powers until the stirrings of the Industrial Revolution.

During the heyday of overseas expansion other seaboard states rose to considerable strength, only to subside to positions commensurate with the force inherent in their European homelands, coupled with such overseas holdings as they were able to retain. Portugal, Netherlands, Denmark, and Sweden are the varied illustrations of this history.

The Industrial Revolution brought new resources into play, both within Europe and as imports from other continents. There followed a corresponding alteration in the political balance. Of the established large states, Spain lagged far behind France in both population and power, while Britain forged somewhat ahead. Their shift in position tallies with the distribution of natural resources on which industrial society is based. Using appropriate resources with exceptional skill, Germany became unified as a leading maritime-manufactural country, and Italy was carried in its train as a runner-up among the Great Powers.

[127]

In East Central Europe, where the scale of the landscape is larger than in the west, several extensive but unstable states were struggling for territory and the power that goes with population and resources. Only two became Great Powers (Fig. 13, p. 120).

Austria, from a fixed coreland on the Danube, added enough land by conquest from the Turks to compare in size with the large states of Western Europe. It was already recognized as a Great Power before the Industrial Revolution began. Thanks to trade routes, coal, and iron, it remained in the running until its *debâcle* at the end of World War I.

Prussia, on the North European Plain, inherited the lands of several districts established during the later Middle Ages as marches on the frontier of Saxony. Like its predecessors, its function was to supplant the Slavic population east of the Elbe River with central Europeans. In the slow process, Prussia developed military power out of proportion to its meager environment, notable for infertile soil. In successive steps it conquered productive lands both east and west of its nucleus. Among them was the Ruhr region, where Europe's richest coal field was later discovered. With its military tradition buttressed by manufactures based upon the industrialized Ruhr, Prussia unified most of Germanic Europe, which then suddenly seized a place as a Great Power.

Russia as a Eurasian Great Power

Russia took its first steps toward Europe while the Atlantic states were still exploring the overseas continents. Two centuries passed and England was becoming industrialized before the Russian state succeeded in annexing territory traditionally European in social structure and way of thinking (Fig. 11, p. 96). By these conquests, and by consciously imitating European ways, Russia made a strong bid to join the family of European nations. The government of the Czars participated in European affairs for two centuries or more, until overthrown during World War I.

The state thus ruled as a member of European political society ultimately extended its western boundary to the Gulf of Bothnia and the Danube delta, incorporating nearly all the northern half of the "shatter belt," and exerting strong influence over most of the remainder. Eastward it reached 250 miles beyond the central Urals, but the rest of its Asiatic possessions had the status of colonies.

[128]

Physical Geography. The physical geography of Russia, even when defined in these restricted terms, contrasts sharply in most respects with that of truly European states. It is almost as large as all of traditional Europe. Perhaps half of the vast area is tundra, stunted forest, and desert. Such lands, of slight value and able to support only a sparse population, hardly exist in Europe. Russian rivers, though large, are ice-covered so much of the year that they are not much good for navigation, and they all lead to ports equally ice-bound or to waters wholly or partly landlocked. Hence Russia lacks important natural incentives to overseas trade. Overland trade is further handicapped by vast distances between regions of contrasting production. Moreover, local exchange between neighboring regions is not reinforced by any world trade-routes crossing the country from terminals outside. Rich deposits of coal and iron, the minerals on which large-scale manufacturing has elsewhere been based, exist in Russia, but separated by more than 200 miles, with no connecting waterway. Their development lagged behind the mining and manufacturing that drew on the better articulated deposits of Europe.

Beyond Russia proper extended its possessions in Siberia, Central Asia, and the Caucasus. This vast territory was colonial, but unlike the colonies of European nations. It was adjacent instead of overseas; it constituted a unit instead of being made up of different, scattered pieces; it was bounded by desert, mountain, or ice-blocked ocean, instead of being accessible to ships. Only in its variety of natural environment and diversity of peoples did the Russian empire resemble the empires of the leading colonial states of the West.

Political Geography. Until at least the eighteenth century the whole area remained in political flux comparable to that of medieval Europe. Since then, some of its boundaries, especially in the west, have continued to fluctuate between wide limits. This is not out of scale with the size of Russia as a whole, but in more narrowly European terms the magnitude is such that it has engulfed or disgorged several border states. Overrunning these European neighbors has given Russia its position as a European Great Power. Yet, compared to the small political units of Europe, where each state clings to naturally marked boundaries or strives to reach them, the union of the vast Russian territory in a single state was anomalous. Besides its outsize area, it had a population two to three times as large as the most populous European nations, and its autocratic and feudal political system retained the machinery that had long before been wholly or largely discarded by states farther west.

During World War I Russia withdrew from European associations, and when hostilities came to a close four or five years later, it had lost all territory on the western border that was not indisputably Russian in population. The government symbolized its attitude by retracting its capital from St. Petersburg (Leningrad), its "window on the Baltic," to Moscow, the original nucleus of the nation in the heart of the continental interior.

Technology and Organization. Before and after this date Russia took advantage of the Transport Revolution, from which no nation stood to gain more. Its large size, its inland location, and the northward or southward flow of rivers in a land where the population stretches from west to east, are disadvantages that the railway and the motor road are admirably fitted to overcome (Fig. 13, p. 120). By the end of the nineteenth century a coarse mesh of rail lines covered the populous triangle between the western boundary and the central Urals, and a single track reached east to the Pacific. Since World War I this skeleton has been extended to tie in outlying areas, as each climatic region was developed for its special products and fitted into exchange economy, and as mineral deposits were turned into mines. Navigation of the air has reinforced the surface pattern of routes in the coreland, and in addition has brought within quick communication the deserts, mountains, and cold lands of the frontiers. Abundant reserves of petroleum make it practicable for Russia to fit into the automotive age, not only on land and in air, but also undersea, submarines being the only serviceable naval craft for a power so nearly landlocked as is the Soviet Union.

In mechanical technology, Soviet Russia has avidly followed the pattern of the Industrial Revolution. Utilization of its varied natural resources on a scale commensurate with their abundance lies outside the range of European experience, however, and the Russians have often found the American modification of European techniques better suited to Russian conditions than the original prototype.

In attempting a new order of society, the Soviet plan derives from the brain of Karl Marx, a European, but not from any European nation. Accordingly, state capitalism has been substituted for private capitalism, an oligarchic "Party" of self-made men for the Czarist oligarchy of hereditary landholders, and local cultures in place of European models in language and the arts. These are generally held to be the antithesis of cautious Marxist experiments being made in Europe. Basically they more nearly resemble the Russian tradition of an absolute, one-man government engaged in holding together, by economic as well as political means, a vast and varied area inhabited by diverse and generally backward peoples.

At the close of World War II Russia was again in occupation of part of the shatter belt, with a boundary on the Baltic nearly 100 miles farther west than ever before, and in the Carpathians, 150 miles. It controls, either as satellites or through military occupation, the entire shatter belt, plus two-fifths of the former German state. This appears to make it once more a European Power, despite the attitude of isolation from the affairs of the occidental world adopted by the Soviet government.

It is, indeed, more than a Great Power of Europe; it stands in the front rank of world states by sheer force of area and population. The technological overturn that brought it into the train of the Western World in methods of using its natural resources, and the political revolution that organized its material and patriotic power as a striking weapon in both war and peace, have made it a Great Power in the terms of 1950. Between present accomplishments and the potential of its environment there remains a wide gap, even though a large fraction of its territory is narrowly limited by harsh climate. No state of peninsular Europe, even with its overseas holdings, can hope to regain the status of a Great Power in the sense that Russia can remain a Great Power.

Great Power Overseas

The United States of America more nearly approximates the traditional European way of life than does the Soviet Union. However, the scale of its area, population, and utilization of resources takes it out of the class of European states. Like Russia, the United States grew up in the time of the Transport Revolution. Its diverse regions were literally bound together with steel rails. Later a web of motor roads and a thick dotting of airfields came to supplement the net of railroads. During the first half of the twentieth century this new-world offshoot of Europe spread its interests to all the continents. Its unwilling but energetic participation in wars of the period, both hatched in Europe, and its current political action in continents far from North America, attest the power position that energetic utilization of its rich natural resources has imposed upon it.

The Commonwealth of Nations is made up of scattered territories and so looks very different on a map from the Soviet Union or the United States. Nevertheless, its combined force is, like theirs, derived from large area, dense populations, and varied resources. Its organizing center on the fringe of Europe and European in tradition, has retained a hold on offshoots in the middle latitudes of North America, South Africa, and Australia-New Zealand that together may fairly be compared to the United States of America. The Commonwealth also includes peoples of South Asia, recalling the Central Asian peoples of the Soviet Union. Finally there are the colonies, source of additional wealth, which are not unlike colonies of other European nations. These elements form an entirely adequate base for Great Power, if they stick together. The Commonwealth as a whole and also its larger subdivisions benefit no less than Russia and the United States from air transport. The subcontinental self-governing dominions profit equally from rapid land transport. The association of units scattered all over the globe was made possible by seafaring, and is unique in its dependence on speedy ocean transport.

Europe as a Nursery

In the past each succeeding era of history has seen Europe cast in the rôle of nursery for advancing social groups. Beginning with very small areas, uniform in climate and resources, and isolated from neighbors, the western tradition has moved into larger spaces, adapted itself to varied climates and landforms, and learned to use a multiplicity of natural resources. In the process, isolation has given way to a worldwide net of communication. Possessing a unique combination of favorable natural conditions, Europeans maintained political dominance and economic leadership in the successive worlds of which they have been a part. Territorial losses occasionally suffered were ultimately regained, along with expansion into new lands.

Discoveries of unknown territory came to an end at the close of the first decade of the twentieth century, when both the North and South Poles were visited. At about the same time the range of controlled human movement was extended to include the air and the undersea. These facts signalize the completion of mankind's exploration of terrestrial space. At the mid-point of the century it has become possible for the first time to view the earth as global in fact, as well as in theory. Every aspect of human life is touched by this magic. .

Men have gained a vision of "one world." The League of Nations and the United Nations have been efforts to realize this vision in a political order encompassing all the world's governments, and operating in global terms over the whole range of economic and social life as well. Both organizations were born of the throes of world wars precipitated in Europe. Their global character raises the question as to where Europe stands in the world of "six seas and seven continents."

The earlier League fell short of its purpose, having failed to obtain the consistent support of both the United States and the Soviet Union. Thus it was reduced to an instrument of European policy with which small sovereignties of other continents were affiliated. It seems symbolic that its seat was in the heart of Europe. In the United Nations organization the most powerful voices come from outside the traditional Europe that once ruled the world (if the Commonwealth of Nations is accepted as largely non-European). By choosing New York as its seat the United Nations underline the strength of their non-European membership. Western society appears to have outgrown the nursery at last, leaving mother Europe to find its new place in a world it no longer guides.

HOW EUROPEAN IS THE WORLD?

The impress of Europe on the larger world began with overseas connections, outcome of the Discoveries, and was deepened by the intensified use of natural resources set in motion with the Industrial Revolution. The current Transport Revolution is bringing all the continents within closer range of each other. Ensuing contacts can lead to deeper etching of the European impress—"one world" cast in the European mold; they can take the Soviet form; or they can continue to run the familiar gamut of associated groups with their too-familiar frictions. History alone can tell which, but some trends are apparent.

Technological Competition

The industrialized, interdependent economic system nurtured in Europe has ramified to every other part of the earth. Minerals in demand, wherever found, become a basis for a mining industry and for trade, as soon as they are made accessible. Many districts were originally opened to obtain minerals. An extreme case is the Congo-Zambesi headwaters of central Africa, tapped by long river and rail lines for the sake of its copper, zinc, uranium, diamonds, tin, cobalt, and lead. These and most other minerals are easily exported, but some mineral deposits, notably coal and iron, have served as the means of fixing the location of large-scale manufactures. Europe was the earliest such center, and thus far all the others have been in the humid middle latitudes of the Northern Hemisphere.

More systematic than the distribution of minerals is the pattern of world climates. In the humid middle latitudes of the Americas, South Africa, and Australia, the descendants of emigrant Europeans have been busily modelling their new countries on the old. Beginning with the exchange of raw materials and foodstuffs from their untapped natural environments for manufactured goods of Europe, they subsequently create factory districts in locations where power, labor, and market favor large-scale production of local or imported raw materials, thereby keeping resources at home and reaping profits from the enhanced value of processed goods. Japan, an old nation in the same climatic belt, industrialized itself by imitating European methods, and afterwards set up factories on mainland Asia. More recently China has altered its home manufactures to take some advantage of machines.

The remaining middle-latitude country, the Soviet Union, is busy adopting the technology of Europe, either directly or by way of North America. While thus seeking technical parity with the Western World, the Soviet government pursues a policy of economic isolation enforced through rigidly-controlled national economy. In Russia, capital is owned and operated by the state, a marked antithesis to the traditional European system of private capital. Outside the fringe of Soviet dictation, no nation has gone to this extreme, although nearly all states are tightening the government rein on economic production and exchange. This contrasts with the *laissez faire* that dominated the immediately preceding centuries of Modern History.

Trade between Europe and the low latitudes was a prime incentive of the Discoveries, and after 450 years, exchange of produce from contrasting climates maintains commerce in vigor. Manufacturing has touched the tropics only lightly. A beginning has been made where heat is tempered by altitude, as in Mexico and southern Brazil. In India mineral resources and ample labor have recently been combined to initiate the factory system in imitation of Europe —the first case in a low-latitude lowland.

National controls intended to accelerate factory production and to keep the products of labor at home have affected world trade. Nevertheless, commerce is still an active and worldwide economic pursuit, because all countries see the need of maintaining trade relations in order to exchange the output of different natural environments, if only to fill gaps in local resources. It is less obvious, but equally true, that the maximum trade passes between the major industrialized areas, because of the high degree of their specialization. Europe remains the largest potential trading region on earth, closely followed by North America, and the traffic across the North Atlantic ranks easily first among the ocean trade routes. This holds not only during wars, but also in times of peace. Economic interdependence arising from utilizing the world's resources where and when wanted was created by Europe, and it persists in the face of dislocations resulting from wars and controlled national economies.

Political Hold

Europe's political grip on the world is slackening. This is not new, although it has been brought to the public attention by the spectacular shift of South Asia from colonial status to autonomy or independence after the end of World War II. The first withdrawal from the European political orbit was that of thirteen North American colonies of Great Britain, just as the Industrial Revolution was taking hold. Independence had spread throughout the Western Hemisphere by the opening of the twentieth century, leaving only small relics of European colonial empires.

East Asia was never incorporated fully into the European political system, and by the middle of the twentieth century most of the special privileges of Europeans that had been imposed were abrogated, including extra-territorial legal status and concessions of territory in "treaty ports." [1] With the defection of South Asia, Europe's political hold in the populous Orient has vanished, or it is replaced by voluntary association, or it rests on the shaky foundation of unresolved rebellion.

Of the colonial areas continental in scale, only Africa remains. Small, scattered holdings include islands and other spots that were critical in the former structure of overseas empire and may retain strategic value. Remnants of once extensive holdings are also scattered and generally low in value besides.

Along with territorial shrinkage of empires, the twentieth century has also witnessed a change of attitude on the part of European states toward their remaining overseas holdings. Large areas in the middle latitudes, peopled by European stock, were already autonomous when the century opened. Their right to withdraw completely from European connections is now unchallenged. The change in political status of British territory in South Asia following World War II, is an extension of the principle of self-determination to low-latitude, non-European peoples which have long possessed a high culture. Some places mandated to European authority at the end of World War I have since become independent nations by a similar peaceful process. Certain colonies under flags other than the British have been given or offered membership in federation with the European state to which they were formerly subject.

Groups less experienced in European ways are increasingly viewed as being under trusteeship, rather than domination, of the holding country. Such an attitude narrows the range of exploitation, by reserving to indigenous inhabitants of "backward regions" some or all of the natural resources. Along with economic protection goes a program to prepare for increasing participation in the local government by representatives of the populace.

Paradoxically the weakening grip of European states on the colonial world is one outcome of the economy introduced by European administrators. As each subject territory has become in-

[1] Subordination of Japan as a consequence of defeat in World War II is presumed to be temporary, and does not refute this statement.

ternally integrated by improved communications and enriched by enhanced use of its resources, intellectual ferment has started that in time leads to breaking or loosening the political tie.

Social Resistance

No change between 1900 and 1950 is more striking than the recrudescence of non-European cultures. The force that has compelled European states to grant autonomy or independence to colonial areas has lately been expressed in a vigorous rejuvenation of an ancient local culture which appeared to be suppressed or extinguished. This commonly follows revival of the local language as a symbol of the whole culture, which in turn becomes a lever to obtain political freedom. East and South Asia provide several notable cases, but the renascence of Indian societies in Middle America expresses the same spirit, although directed against local, independent governments made up of people tracing European descent, rather than against European nations.

Soviet Russia reverses the process by highlighting the language and art of the minorities within the Union, while basically altering the use of the land and its resources to conform to occidental, usually European, practice. It may be that all these upsurgings of local cultures and insistence on political separation make the unremitting advance of European technology and economy more acceptable to non-European peoples.

As 1950 approaches, Europe, half a century earlier the apparent political mistress of the earth, as well as its economic mainspring and social pattern, finds itself beset with opposition and apostasy— both overseas and on the adjacent Eurasian continent. Much of the body of technology, organization, and way of thinking that originated in Europe has been adopted in other parts of the earth, but generally with modifications, and sometimes with differences so marked that the European source is hard to trace.

THE BASES OF EUROPE'S PROSPECT

Viewed as a composite of natural conditions, Europe compares favorably with other chief centers of the world's population.

Inherent Advantages

It is subcontinental in size at a period when technical advances favor large units. Its climate includes most of the varieties to be found within the humid middle latitudes—contrasts advantageous for trade and travel. Except in the far northeast there are no climatic extremes. Even if the Mediterranean coast of Africa is included, the desert margin not far inland sets the limit to "Europe." No area of equal size on earth is so favored in climate—both in its variety and in its suitability for human life under conditions of the present day.

European soils inherently range from high-grade to low, but none of the most fertile types occur except in spots. Nearly all respond well to careful management, however, and sedulous attention over many decades enables them to produce more now than they did in their natural state. Soils too infertile to use for crops or grazing are planted to productive forests. Those which have deteriorated from wartime ravages can be rehabilitated without undue effort.

Despite favorable soil and climate, Europe has not been quite self-sustaining in food, because of its large industrial population. Hence it must import farm surpluses of other continents.

Minerals of most kinds are still available and widely distributed, in spite of heavy drain by manufacturing industries and by wars. Two of the three most critical soil fertilizers are present in large quantities, and the third can be manufactured from local resources. Rich coal fields occur from Scotland to Poland, and ample iron ores for steelmaking lie not far from the coal. The Western economic order since the Industrial Revolution has been based on these two minerals. As various metals have been increasingly used to make alloy steel, European self-sufficiency has diminished, because several have to be brought from outside. This is not difficult to do, the amounts needed being small and ocean shipping inexpensive.

The main ingredients of the chemical industry are at hand in generous amounts—salt, sulfur, lime, and coal. Farmed forests can provide cellulose for plastics and paper indefinitely, although probably not in sufficient quantity to meet the annual requirements of the factories.

[138]

Most of the commoner ores, notably those of lead, zinc, copper, and aluminum, are mined in modest quantities, and in a number of different places. The mineral most conspicuously short is petroleum. There is probably little uranium or thorium, the minerals at present used for atomic fission. Tin is nearly exhausted.

Lacks of all kinds can ordinarily be made up by importation. Europe pays for its imported food and raw materials with manufactured exports. The cheapest form of transport is by sea, and all of Europe faces the open ocean or adjacent seas. So far, it appears that trade grows as the other continents expand their manufactures, but this may not continue indefinitely. Meantime, political restrictions on trade continue to hamper free movement of goods.

In natural resources, Europe probably remains the richest area *of its size* on earth. The population is large without being excessive, and hard-working. As each section has taken its place as a manufacturing region, its population strikes a balance between births and deaths, or perhaps falls off slightly. Gross overpopulation therefore is unlikely to occur.

Position on the Globe

When Europe is compared to other parts of the earth, its relative position is clarified. If it lay five degrees farther south (Fig. 14, p. 124), it would reach from the Arctic Circle nearly to the Tropic of Cancer, thus encompassing the middle latitudes of the Northern Hemisphere. As it is, the warm water of the Mediterranean Sea and the Gulf Stream offsets its far northern location, to bring all but the tip into the domain of middle-latitude climates. All the lands widely considered to be suitable bases for existing or potential Great Powers, including China, lie within this belt and in this hemisphere.

Position in Eurasia. While usually called a continent, Europe is physically a small part of Eurasia, the largest land mass on earth, being merely one of five marginal projections of that vast continent (Fig. 2, p. 6). The three smallest of the five are peninsulas reaching southward and lying wholly or largely within the low latitudes. Each of them is sharply separated from the core of the continent by highland or desert or both. The remaining two, Europe and China, lie mainly in humid middle latitudes, and are larger than the others.[1] They are also less cut off from the interior. Europe, particularly, lies open to the heart of the continent; in the south by way of interconnecting basins, and in the north along a gently undulating plain, ridged but not interrupted by the Ural Mountains. China ranks first in population, with India and Europe second and third. The average density of Europe's population is somewhat less than that of the oriental areas. More important, Europe has developed a greater variety of natural resources with corresponding additional sources of livelihood. Of the five, Europe stands in much the best economic position.

In area, the vast core of Eurasia outclasses any of its bordering bulges. The Soviet Union incorporates much of the interior and occupies a sixth of the earth's land surface. The part west of the Urals (sometimes called Russia-in-Europe) is nearly as large as Europe itself. Much of this Eurasian core is rendered useless by dry or cold climates. Perhaps ten per cent of the desert can be irrigated, and a forest crop can be grown on part of the cold lands. The more productive remainder is not so rich as most of Europe's farmland, because the growing season is short in the north and rain is unreliable in the south. The mineral wealth of the entire vast Soviet domain is incompletely known, because in many regions it has not yet been thoroughly prospected. It is believed to include most of the minerals found in Europe, plus alloy metals, fissionable minerals, and petroleum.

Europe is not set off from the continental interior by any natural barrier, because the grain of the country runs east-west rather than north-south (Fig. 11, p. 96). A broad lowland passage along the Black Sea is bordered on the north by a crescent of low mountains (the Carpathians) which lie within Europe but present their convex front to the Russian plain in the form of steep slopes. North of the mountains five hundred miles of plain extend to the Baltic Sea. In this belt lies a huge morass, the Pripet Marsh, a barrier equal to or surpassing the mountains. But wide-open gateways of firm ground flank it: to the north the coastal lowland; to the south the Carpathian piedmont, a segment of the most densely populated part of western Eurasia—a belt that reaches from the Rhine-Scheldt

[1] Defining Europe as the truly peninsular part west of the traditional lands of Russia, and China as China Proper plus Manchuria, makes the two areas approximately equal: Europe—2,092,000 square miles; China—1,923,000 square miles.

Delta to Kiev on the Dnieper River. The mountains have been crisscrossed by routes from early times, and railroads now traverse both them and the marshes. Belts of climate and associated natural conditions (water supply, soils, vegetation, and animal life) cross the boundary with no perceptible change.

The distinction between the two worlds appears when the natural and cultural character of Europe is compared with that of interior Eurasia, each area considered as a whole. The marked contrast between typical European geography and equally typical inland geography then appears. It follows that any division *line* drawn through the border zone is arbitrary. More properly the frontier is a belt through which run several kinds of transitions: the break between Roman-German culture and Greek-Slavic culture; the broad span where hill-bordered lowlands on or near salt water give way to featureless inland plains; the coarse versus fine mesh of transport routes; the dominance of continental over marine climate; the political boundary of Russia. The least enduring of these is the political boundary, but for that reason it is also the most indicative of current trends. In this study Europe is loosely defined as reaching to the eastern political boundary of cultural units stamped with the European impress. Whether or not these units are sovereign states is less important than the tenacity with which they hold fast to their western culture. A boundary line drawn according to this definition leaves to Europe the borderlands that drain into the Baltic and the Danube.

Position in the Atlantic Basin. Far to the west of Europe is the transatlantic shore of the North American continent, a land-mass second only to Eurasia in combined size and resources (Fig. 14, p. 124). In several ways it resembles Eurasia. Its northland is so cold that products are confined to timber and minerals, and nearly half of the remaining interior is desert or semi-arid. Its only large area of dense population faces the Atlantic, just as does populous western Eurasia.

The three thousand miles of ocean between the two continents maintained a barrier of ignorance until European navigators broke it down. Each succeeding advance in transportation has reduced the separating character of the ocean. Now the North Atlantic has become the world's most-used sea route, taking from four to a dozen days for the crossing, while air passengers and freight vault it in a few hours. Europe thus finds itself closely and continuously in contact with North America.

Discovery of North America by Europe, occupation and settlement by Europeans, and introduction of the European way of life, have all been facilitated by similarity in natural environment, particularly in the half of the continent that lies between the Gulf of Mexico and Hudson Bay. Humid middle-latitude climates and soils made it possible to grow European crops and raise European livestock. Rich deposits of coal and iron favored large-scale manufacturing. Navigable lakes and rivers carried waterborne commerce far inland. It is not surprising that the huge lowland has become the nearest counterpart to Europe to be found anywhere on earth.

The restless habit of Europeans to push their way into new lands came naturally to their American descendants, always conscious of the frontier at the western edge of their homeland. The process of occupying a continent was greatly accelerated by improvements in transportation brought into being by the Industrial Revolution. After 1800 settlement spread so rapidly that threats of fragmentation were averted. The whole of North America except its low-latitudes fell into two nations, near kin in origin and hardly distinguishable from each other in manner of living. The combined area of the two states is about four-fifths as large as the territory of Soviet Russia, and more than thrice the size of Europe.[1] The living level of their population was higher than Europe's even before the world wars.

Europe in Between

As the twentieth century approaches its midpoint, Europe finds itself between the two parts of the earth that combine to the best advantage certain critical earth conditions: middle-latitude climates, with associated advantages of fertile or fertilizable soils, suitability for the most prized staple crops and livestock, and useful forests; rich and varied mineral deposits, including the keys to high technological attainment, both existent and prospective; such abundance of total resources as to preclude any immediate gross overpopulation; location in the northern hemisphere, where most

[1] Soviet Union—8,708,000 square miles.
North America—7,053,000 square miles.
Europe—2,092,000 square miles.

[142]

of the world's land and people are; large size, both absolutely and in territorial organization.

As the area in between, Europe shares all the advantages of its neighbors except the last. The wealth and variety of its natural resources can be measured roughly by the high productivity and the dense or moderate population in almost every district. No equal area on earth is farmed so advantageously, considering yield both per acre and per capita, and including forests. Its mineral deposits have been more thoroughly prospected than those of Russia and Canada, and they promise a long period of continued production. Europe's total natural resources, after centuries of utilization, are not inferior to the total in each of the flanking areas in ratio to size, and they compare favorably, regardless of size.

Europe stands in the best location of the three for interchange of goods, being at the focus of ocean routes and at the gateway to interior Eurasia. Several European countries have taken steps toward the Marxian views adopted by the Soviet government as a way of life, while holding fast to essentials of the traditional and little-altered order of the United States and Canada. Thus treading the middle path may bring it to a position better adapted to the needs of the times than the extreme viewpoints of its neighbors.

"Space" in Europe

Most of Europe's weaknesses in the prospect of the future can be stated in terms of space. It is much smaller than either North America beyond the sea or Russia adjacent on the continent. Fortunately it contains little wasteland. But extensive wilderness is not altogether a liability. It is a potential source of mineral wealth, and it offers a means of defense against surface operations in case of war. Europe's physical attachment to the Soviet lands combines with its middle location to place it in the path of jet propulsion and atomic bombing, no matter how eagerly its people may desire to stay out of a major war. Its factories, busy turning its abundant natural resources into goods that can be used by belligerents, make it a likely target in case of any war of large extent.

While there are dangers inherent in its geography, Europe is far from negligible. A subcontinent, richly endowed and experienced in making use of its natural advantages, it is one of the few parts of the earth fitted to play a leading rôle in the next decades. Unfortunately, it speaks with many tongues, and its intention and its determination are lost in confusion of conflicting sounds. Europe as an entity does not exist. In a fluid world it remains a rigid patchwork of states, held fast in a vise of national egotisms which solidified long ago.

Its social structure stems from the world of Classical Antiquity (Chapter I), partially remolded in the crucible of the Dark Ages (Chapter II), and further modified in some regions at later times of ferment, most notably the Industrial Revolution (Chapter IV). Its political frame was made to suit a society living almost wholly by farming, with a trickle of slow-moving trade, and a few townsful of craftsmen. The political map of European sovereignties has become increasingly anachronistic with every improvement in transport and communication.

The economic order alone has progressed with the times, spreading a web of ever denser and speedier interchange across political boundaries and penetrating the fastnesses of social isolation. Here and there a customs union has been a forerunner of political unification, although generally confined within the territorial limits of a single language.

More commonly cartels of "big business" have crossed political lines to produce and market goods that can be handled only by joining natural resources from different countries, such as iron ore and coal to make steel, bauxite and water-power to make aluminum, timber and nitrates to make plastics. Cartels were in existence before World War I, and after each conflict they have again emerged in spite of being ostensibly broken up by the state of war. Apparently they are irrepressible for long in a subcontinent where the patterns of political organization and economic requirements are sharply discordant. Yet they make little headway against the political cleavage that formulizes Europe's division into rival social groups. Political boundaries increase the cost and complicate the utilization, in combination, of Europe's total resources. The normal economic organization of the European endowment is distorted by being forced to conform to the pattern of sovereign states. This results from numberless legal restrictions, such as tariffs, subsidies, monetary systems (including banking), and commercial treaties.

Where cartels have been most successful, they have sometimes dictated the action of governments, or have become instruments of ruthless political power. On these grounds also they are an unsatisfactory substitute for political authority. Their existence has not prevented the brutalities of recent years that have raised to white heat national hatreds which seemed largely forgotten when the twentieth century opened.

The political units into which Europe remains divided, many of them tiny and none large, are tempting morsels for voracious power. Twice Germany has undertaken to unify Europe by conquest, only to end in failure. Already since the close of World War II, several states along the eastern margin of Europe have been sucked out of the European political and economic world and into the Russian orbit. To the extent that these withdrawals from Europe become permanent, European predominance will suffer. Today less territory is incontestably European than at any time since the later Middle Ages.

ALTERNATIVE COURSES FOR THE FUTURE

Any attempt to indicate the course of coming events in Europe would be foolhardy. Opposed forces within and without are clashing daily and the pattern of tomorrow is being thereby fashioned bit by bit. The design promises to be complex; its elements alone can be indicated. They suggest alternative possibilities, one of which may take precedence. Or the outcome may be the mixed result of a contest between them.

The European peninsula may perhaps be absorbed by the Great Power seated in the Eurasian interior. Conquest would be a kind of amalgamation not unknown to Europe, but this would be conquest on a scale grander than has ever been conceived within strictly European limits. Every such attempt is sure to be contested by the Europeans themselves, by the Commonwealth of Nations with its island center on the edge of Europe, and by such power as resides in America. Resistance can be expected to increase with distance from the Russian base of expansion.

As a second alternative, Europe may be partitioned between the Soviet system and the West. Partition, like absorption, is a familiar European practice. The military line drawn at the end of World War II between the Russian Zone and the Western Zones follows closely the ancient cleavage between Germanic Europe, Romanized by the end of Dark Ages, and Slavic Europe, which was overlaid in the later Middle Ages and through German channels with North European culture, containing by then only fragmentary Roman elements (Fig. 11, p. 96). Originally defined in 1945 for temporary military occupation only, it soon after became an administrative line with an undefined future, and it could be converted into a political boundary assumed to be permanent. So entrenched, it would cut in two the German culture area, thus conflicting with nationalism, which has been the chief emotional force underlying western politics for two centuries.

Federation of Europe into a single Great Power is the objective of many idealists and some practical politicians. The survey of Europe's aggregate strength (in the preceding section) makes it clear that federation would consolidate power so concentrated as to be matched elsewhere only in much larger areas. The unique combination of favorable conditions on which Europeans based leadership of the world in the past has not been outclassed by the contemporary world, if only it is utilized as a unit. Internal unification is one of the oldest and most persistent European practices. It has been most successful within a narrow cultural range.

Since World War II, efforts have been made to integrate units long separated by social and political barriers, but clearly in need of association for their mutual benefit, both economic and political. As a result of these efforts, three political associations have been created.

The most inclusive in its coverage is a plan for progressive economic and political union of three small sovereignties at and near the mouth of the Rhine: Belgium, Netherlands, and Luxemburg, for which the portmanteau name Benelux has been coined (Fig. 13, p. 120). Several things predispose to its success. They share the lowest Rhineland, zone of contact between the busiest river system on earth and the world focus of ocean trade; they serve as middlemen between central Europe and the world overseas. They possess valuable reciprocal resources, particularly coal and iron ore. Their histories have been similar, and at times they have been politically unified. Their current, independent governments are nearly alike in form and operation. At present their organization is being implemented in economic matters. Later on, steps will be directed toward closer political affiliation. The whole plan will require several years, in order to cushion shocks to the economy that are inevitable in a change of political pattern.

A second proposal provides for more narrowly limited coöperation spread over a much larger area. In a sense it is an outgrowth of Benelux, because the three members of that group joined with Britain and France at the Belgian capital to prepare for a military union. The treaty they signed at Brussels provides for economic and cultural coöperation, and joint military action in case of attack. It envisages unity of command, and so differs from ordinary treaties of alliance. By marshalling in peacetime the total armed force of the states involved into a single operating unit, it creates joint utilization of the space and resources of the signatories. Inclusion of France and Britain in this plan for unified control of armies, navies, and air forces rests it upon the largest aggregation of power now existing in Eurasia outside the Soviet Union. Tentative agreement on the division of command has been announced.

A third proposal for coördinate action brings Western Europe into association with Canada and the United States of America in the Atlantic Pact, signed, but not ratified, as these words are being written. To the states joined in the Western Union are added all the independent, Atlantic-facing countries of Europe except Eire and Spain. For good measure Italy has joined. In form a defensive alliance, the North Atlantic Security Alliance provides a frame for extending to the entire Atlantic Basin any desired degree of military organization.

Many hurdles confront comprehensive federation. Separate states persist, not only from momentum, but also because of continuing regional unities, among them an unmistakable nuclear core, easy access to the core, uniform or neatly reciprocal resources, a common history, the same language. Once established, a state is shaped by its boundaries: foreign policy is based in part on the land and its resources and deficiencies; business is adjusted to raw materials, labor, power, and market available within the state; pride in national sovereignty is aroused; inherited suspicion, passion, and hatred of outlanders, generated by centuries of warfare, have been reinvigorated by the unhappy history of the decade ending as these words are written.

The fourth alternative for the future is to patch the European structure, when and where it threatens to disintegrate. This practice is more commonly followed than any of the others. In default of a positive or comprehensive program, attempts must be made to solve each problem by such piecemeal expedients as happen to be within the imaginative and material grasp of the threatened areas.

Each of the four alternatives finds precedents in Europe's history. The entire world has a heavy stake in Europe's future. A region of such imposing past importance and present capacity is bound to remain a critical and an inescapable factor in the lives of coming generations, whether they live there or in other parts of the earth.

Useful Geographic Tools
and Materials

T his book is addressed primarily to college classes in both European History and Western Civilization. The geographic background it pictures is presented as briefly as possible, in recognition of the wealth of material that presses to be read in history courses, both introductory and advanced, and in the cognate courses on Western society. Such a book as this, itself intended for supplementary reading, is hardly the place to cite many additional references. Instead it seems desirable to indicate the geographic tools and materials likely to be most useful to students and teachers in familiarizing themselves with further details of the geography underlying European history. This will enable readers who find satisfaction in visualizing the stage on which the drama of history is enacted, to pursue European geography as far as they may care to go. The items listed are annotated to suggest their character and their utility.

CARTOGRAPHIC AIDS

A globe and an atlas are indispensable for visualizing the earth-scene of the human events that become history.

Globes

The globe occupies a unique place among geographic tools, because it is the only means of representing the earth or the continents without distortion. Most globes are made to show states and their possessions. The political units are useful in historical study, even when they stand alone; but the value of political boundaries is enhanced many fold if they are superposed on some aspect of natural environment. The usual groundwork of such globes combines relief of the lands and drainage lines. The ordinary political globe is also cluttered with many names of places. For legibility the best globe is one which leaves off all but the most important cities. Flat maps in the atlas are drawn on a larger scale, and show places more clearly than is possible on a spherical surface of practicable size. Globes that depict relief are admirably untrammelled with place-names—another point in their favor.

Large globes are expensive, but the well-equipped history classroom will make good use of one sixteen or more inches in diameter. Six- or eight-inch globes are not beyond the individual purse, for home study. The mounting of a globe is an item in its cost. The most useful is the cheapest—a simple cradle in which the globe rests free, so that it can be picked up and turned about in the hands. Most map-making firms include globes in their catalogs. American firms are listed below:

Weber Costello Company, Chicago Heights, Illinois. Globes are their specialty.
Rand McNally & Company, Chicago, New York, and San Francisco.
Denoyer-Geppert, 5235 Ravenswood Ave., Chicago.
A. J. Nystrom & Company, 3333 Elston Avenue, Chicago.
The George F. Cram Co., Inc., Indianapolis 7, Indiana.
C. S. Hammond and Company, 88 Lexington Ave., New York 16.

Maps and Atlases

Flat maps are the only practicable means of showing details of space relations and differences that come with passage of time. Most history textbooks include a few maps in black-and-white, their favorite theme being territorial changes. The insufficiency of textbook maps is recognized in the widespread use of a historical atlas made up of colored maps, and owned by each member of the class or reserved in the library. While most maps in these atlases are exclusively political, some portray economic or social patterns, and a few suggest relief of the land by hachures or even by contours. Where relief and some aspect of the culture pattern appear on the same map, something of the historical geography can be deduced. Apart from relief, historical atlases do not attempt to show climate, soils, or any of the other aspects of nature that condition human events, either as separate "geographic" maps or in relation to particular moments of history.

Nearly all the maps illustrating the present book undertake to suggest landforms and drainage, and several portray climate or vegetation or mineral deposits significant to specified periods of history. Adequate coverage of all environmental conditions can be found only in certain atlases intended primarily for courses in geography, but also well suited to the study of history. The political and economic facts shown in such atlases are confined to the period of their publication, but the aspects of the environment they present are valid for all periods of history. Two such atlases are especially useful:

GOODE, J. Paul, *School Atlas* (Chicago, Rand McNally & Co., 1947).
BARTHOLOMEW, John, *The Oxford Advanced Atlas* (London, Oxford University Press, 1936). This atlas, being a British publication, has a higher ratio of European maps than the American Goode's atlas.

A graphic, stylized representation of Europe's surface features is separately published, with a descriptive text:

LOBECK, A. K., *Physiographic Diagram of Europe,* 19x24 inches and 8½ x11 (New York, The Geographical Press, Columbia University).

TEXTUAL MATERIALS

All geographies include maps, supplementing and illustrating the textual presentation. Geography books valuable to the student of European history fall into two general categories, regional and topical or systematic. Regional geography may be studied at any order of magnitude. Commonly a continent, a sub-continent, or a country is taken as a subject for regional analysis. Topics in geography cover a wide range, and many of them throw light on history. Only a few of the more illuminating are mentioned in the following lists.

Regional Geography

No book on European geography can be recommended without a statement as to what it includes, because geographies of Europe vary widely in coverage, in topics treated, and in organization. Like geographic atlases, they are usually confined to the period of their publication. Because the natural environment is far more stable than human society, what they have to say about it holds good for all periods of history. What they say about human geography enlarges the reader's understanding of recent history and current events.

Europe as a Whole. No book treats Europe as a unit, beyond an introductory chapter prefacing more detailed chapters on the regional subdivisions of the continent. The following selection is limited to works in English.

MacMunn, Nora E., and Coster, Geraldine, *Europe: A Regional Geography* (Oxford, Clarendon Press, n.d. [after 1919]). A graphic portrayal in non-technical language.

McConnell, W. R., *Geography of Lands Overseas* (Chicago, Rand, McNally, 1948). Written for high-school classes in geography, the six chapters on Europe and adjacent Asia are not too elementary for classes in introductory college history.

Shackleton, Margaret R., *Europe: A Regional Geography* (London, Longmans, Green, 1934). An excellent and detailed work that presupposes acquaintance with the simpler technical terms of physical geography.

Newbigin, Marion I., *A New Regional Geography of the World* (New York, Harcourt, Brace, 1929). Briefer than the foregoing, and couched in non-technical language. Only eight chapters deal with Europe.

Wright, John K., *The Geographical Basis of European History* (New York, Holt, 1928). A quick survey of European and bordering lands, written with the student of history in mind.

European Regions or Countries. Studies similar to the foregoing, but confined to parts of the continent, are correspondingly detailed in portrayal of both the natural environment and the human occupance of the areas under discussion. They vary widely in emphasis, in literary merit, and in usefulness. Most of them are intended for advanced students, conversant with the principles and language of geography.

Laborde, E. D., *A Geography of Western Europe* (London, University of London Press, 1928).

Newbigin, Marion L., *Southern Europe*. (London, Methuen, 1932).

Partsch, Joseph, *Central Europe* (New York, Appleton, 1903).

Woods, E. G., *The Baltic Region* (London, Methuen, 1932).

Ormsby, Hilda, *France; A Regional and Economic Geography* (New York, Dutton, 1931).

Demangeon, A., *The British Isles* (London, Heinemann, 1939).

The pertinent volumes of *La Géographie Universelle*, published in Paris by Colin, together cover the continent more completely and more thoroughly than does any combination of works in English.

Volume I (1927) DEMANGEON, A., *Les Îles Britanniques.*
    II (1927) DEMANGEON, A., *Belgique, Pays Bas, Luxembourg.*
    III (1933) ZIMMERMAN, Maurice, *États Scandinaves.*
    IV¹ (1930)⎫
    IV² (1931)⎭ DE MARTONNE, Emm., *Europe Centrale.*
    V (1932) D'ALMEIDA, P. Camena, *États de la Baltique; Russie.*
    VI¹ (1942) DE MARTONNE, Emm., *La France, Physique.*
    VI² (1946) DEMANGEON, A., *La France.*
    VII¹ (1934) SORRE, Max. et SION, Jules, *Méditerranée.*
    VII² (1934) SION, Jules et CHATAIGNEAU, Y., *Méditerranée.*

Topical Geography

The topic in geography presumably of most interest to the student of history is historical geography. Most of the works listed in this section and some of those listed below under the heading, *Special Topics,* bear directly on history.

Historical Geography. Titles specified as being historical geography of Europe are few, and areal coverage is spotty. Their subject-matter lies closer to the content of this book than do general geographies. No two have the same objective or organization. The most usual type presents the sweep of history in chronological order. The result is specialized history, in which geography is accented instead of being neglected, as it is in most histories. These studies in turn omit or minimize other aspects of the complete historical picture.

EAST, Gordon, *An Historical Geography of Europe* (London, Methuen, 1935). Regional monographs, rather than a comprehensive recital.
MACKINDER, Halford J., *Britain and the British Seas* (New York, Appleton, 1902). A survey of the world setting of the British Islands from early times.
KERMACK, W. R., *Historical Geography of Scotland* (Edinburgh, W. & A. K. Johnston, 1913, *rev.,* 1926).

Special Topics. Some studies are limited to a particular period of history, the character of which influences the selection of topics.

SEMPLE, Ellen C., *The Geography of the Mediterranean Region* (New York, Holt, 1931). Confined to the Classical Period of History; for that time and place, invaluable.
JONES, L. Rodwell, and BRYAN, Patrick, *North America* (London, Methuen, 1924, *rev.,* 1928). The conditions of ocean navigation at the time of the Discoveries are clearly stated in the first chapter of this work.

In this category of period analyses, two books, both by Central Europeans, discuss Europe in the light of its geography and history, each at a critical moment of the twentieth century.

VOGEL, Walther, *Das neue Europa und seine historisch-geographische Grundlagen* (Bonn and Leipzig, Schroeder, 1921-23). 2 vols.

FISCHER, Eric, *The Passing of the European Age* (Cambridge, Mass., Harvard University Press, 1943, *rev.*, 1948). Opinions about contemporary Europe, based on its geography and its past history.

In a very different topical frame, two books present concepts of the place of energy as a basic earth resource of human society— ideas perhaps not entirely acceptable, but full of suggestions to the thoughtful student of the interwoven fabric of history and geography.

FAIRGRIEVE, James, *Geography and World Power* (New York, Dutton, 1915, *rev.*, 1942).

ZIMMERMAN, Erich W., *World Resources and Industries* (New York, Harper, 1933).

BIBLIOGRAPHIC AIDS

The student who wishes to range further into European geography will find references in the foregoing books. Outstanding bibliographical aids are listed below.

WRIGHT, John K., and PLATT, Elizabeth T., *Aids to Geographical Research* (New York, Columbia University Press, 1947).

Bibliographie Géographique Internationale, annually (Paris, Colin; New York, American Geographical Society, 1923, *ff.*).

Current Geographical Publications, monthly (New York, American Geographical Society, 1937, *ff.*). A record of acquisitions to the library of the American Geographical Society.

Index

(Figures in bold-faced type indicate pages on which maps occur.)

(1)